LENT AND EASTER
with MARY

THOMAS J. CRAUGHWELL

PARACLETE PRESS
BREWSTER, MA

Lent and Easter with Mary

2008 First printing

Copyright © 2008 by Thomas J. Craughwell
ISBN: 978-1-55725-561-7

Scripture quotations are taken from *The Catholic Edition of the Revised Standard Version of the Bible*, copyright 1965, 1966 by the Division of Christian Education of the National Council of the Churches of Christ in the United States of America. Used by permission.

Library of Congress Cataloging-in-Publication Data

Craughwell, Thomas J., 1956-
  Lent and Easter with Mary / Thomas J. Craughwell.
    p. cm.
  ISBN 978-1-55725-561-7
1. Mary, Blessed Virgin, Saint—Prayers and devotions.
2. Mary, Blessed Virgin, Saint—Miscellanea. 3. Lent--Miscellanea. 4. Easter—Miscellanea. 5. Mary, Blessed Virgin, Saint—Biography. I. Title.
  BX2160.23.C4 2008
  242'.34--dc22
                                    2007040187

10 9 8 7 6 5 4 3 2 1

Published by Paraclete Press
Brewster, Massachusetts
www.paracletepress.com

Printed in the United States of America

CONTENTS

INTRODUCTION

"The Virgin Mary has been more of an inspiration to more people than any other woman who ever lived." That's a pretty sweeping statement, but since it was made by the late Jaroslav Pelikan, Sterling Professor of History at Yale University and lifelong student of the impact of Jesus and Mary on every facet of human history for the last two thousand years, we can assume that it is correct. Mary's influence over the hearts and minds and imaginations of believers is remarkable and humbling. Her name is mentioned in prayer countless times every day. She has inspired more works of art—from the works of old masters to holy cards—and more musical compositions—from soaring polyphonic Masses to May Crowning hymns—than any other woman in history. And in spite of the popularity of St. Joseph, St. Anthony, and St. Jude, when people believe they have had a mystical encounter, they invariably claim to see the Virgin Mary.

Mary inspires love and confidence to a degree that surpasses all other saints. We identify with her because she was as human as us; she was a daughter and a wife and a mother; she knew heart-piercing sorrows and great joys. Because of all these elements, we feel close to her, but because, unlike us, she was entirely sinless, we know that Mary is very close to God.

When the church wishes to honor a divine mystery or a saint, it does so liturgically by assigning a day when the mystery or the saint will be recalled and celebrated at Mass. Secular society does the same thing when it remembers anniversaries of important events. This book draws upon both of those traditions.

Every saint has a feast day, but one could argue that the entire calendar belongs to Mary. Literally each day of the year marks a different feast of Our Lady.

If you are interested, the complete list is available online (although every year it seems to migrate to a different website). In most cases these feasts of Mary are local commemorations that call to mind a dedication of a Marian shrine, a miracle wrought through Mary's intercession at some point in history, or even a significant moment in her life as recorded in tradition or the Gospels—such as the day she married St. Joseph, or the night the Holy Family fled to Egypt to escape King Herod.

As lovely as it is to contemplate that every day Catholics somewhere in the world are celebrating a feast of Our Lady, a little digging in a good library reveals that Mary's influence even pervades the secular world. Each day of the year is not just a feast day of the Blessed Mother, it is also an anniversary of a Mary-related event in art, music, politics, film, education, literature—even sports. But recording these events, as I've done here, is not an exercise in collecting trivia, it is an expression of a great truth: We who love Mary want her to be with us in everything that we do. And she is. For example, it is reassuring, even inspiring, to learn that when Rose Hawthorne Lathrop (the daughter of author Nathaniel Hawthorne) needed reliable, compassionate nurses to help run her cancer ward, she turned to Mary for help. College football fans know that Knute "the Rock" Rockne made Notre Dame's team a powerhouse by introducing them to the forward pass and the shift formation, but did you know that the Rock was not only loyal to Notre Dame the university, but also devoted to Notre Dame the Queen of Heaven? If you think Mary and politics don't mix, consider Our Lady of the Thirty-Three: In 1825, before thirty-three Uruguayan patriots led their country's independence movement, they knelt before a statue of the Blessed Virgin asking for her help and her blessing upon their people. After Uruguay became a sovereign state, the new government hailed Mary as their liberator and national patron. Then there is Renaissance master Raphael, who in his short but dazzling twenty-year career demonstrated his love for Mary by painting at least twenty-one sublime images of the Virgin and Child.

Every page of this book, then, directs your attention to an event when Mary stepped into the picture. And since the only way to grow in love for Mary, to draw closer to her, and to imitate her virtues is through the spiritual life, each entry ends with a prayer adapted from the Bible, the liturgy, or the writings of saints and popes, as well as classic, well-loved prayers that Christians have addressed to the Mother of God for centuries.

Mary is the perfect companion during the holy seasons of Lent and Easter. Lent emphasizes her role as the refuge of sinners, the comforter of the afflicted, and the help of Christians—all titles found in the Litany of the Blessed Virgin. Lent is also the time of year when we try to direct our mind to contemplation of the passion of Christ—and once again, Mary is our ideal companion. On that first Good Friday she was among the faithful few who followed our Lord on the road to Calvary, stood at the foot of the cross as he died, and then received his body into her arms. This is the origin of devotion to Mary as the Mother of Sorrows, grieving for the suffering and death of her son, and for the sins of the world that wounded him.

On Easter morning our companionship with Mary begins on a different note: the Mother of Sorrows is transformed into the joyful Queen of Heaven, as the ancient antiphon "Regina Coeli" proclaims. From Incarnation to Resurrection, Mary was an intimate participant and witness to Christ's work that brought salvation to the world. After the forty sad, solemn days of Lent, the church gives us forty exultant days of Easter to give thanks and be glad that Christ lives, hell is vanquished, and death has lost its sting. And once again, Mary's Litany offers us themes for Easter that reflect her elation and ours—she is the seat of wisdom, the gate of heaven, the cause of our joy.

Two thousand years ago, as she stood outside the home of her elderly cousin Elizabeth, Mary prophesied, "All generations shall call me blessed." Through the centuries, for the part she played in our salvation, for the special graces God bestowed upon her, for the favors she grants to all of us who call upon her for help, every generation has indeed acclaimed Mary as blessed. And she for her part has blessed us by extending her influence to every human endeavor.

LENT AND EASTER
with MARY

ASH WEDNESDAY
Our Lady calls for prayer, sacrifice, and penance

At Lourdes, France, in 1858 Mary called for, "Penance! Penance! Penance!" Then she told Bernadette Soubirous, "Pray to God for sinners."

At Fátima, Portugal, in 1917 Mary instructed Lúcia dos Santos and her cousins, Jacinta and Francisco Marto, "Sacrifice yourselves for sinners."

At Beauraing, Belgium, in 1932 Mary asked five children, "Do you love my son? Do you love me? Then offer yourself up for me." And she made this promise, "I shall convert sinners."

Each Lent is a fresh opportunity for us to turn away from our old sins, failings, and bad habits, to renew our spiritual life, and turn again toward God. But we can't do it alone—we need God's grace. So it is comforting to know that as we progress through Lent we can call upon Mary to support us with her prayers.

The messages she brought to Lourdes, Fatima, and Beauraing are a blueprint for Lent and for every other season of the year. Prayer—both private prayer and the Mass and parish devotions—strengthens and intensifies our relationship with God. Sacrifice overcomes our selfishness. Penance teaches us self-control and sorrow for our sins.

But Mary also asks us to look beyond ourselves and practice a kind of spiritual charity or compassion by praying and making reparation for a world full of people who have turned away from God. This Lent, unite your prayers with Mary, that God's grace will transform your heart and the hearts of people across the world.

**We fly to thy patronage,
O holy Mother of God;
despise not our petitions in our necessities,
but deliver us always from all dangers,
O glorious and Blessed Virgin. Amen.**

Mary Ward is falsely imprisoned for heresy, 1631

I n England during the time when Mary Ward was growing up, to attend Mass and receive the Catholic sacraments was a crime; to receive a priest into your house was a crime; to give your child a Catholic education was a crime; and to refuse to attend Protestant services was a crime. Yet the Ward family remained steadfast Catholics, sheltering disguised priests in their home and practicing their faith privately. Mary wanted to enter the religious life, but all the convents had been shut and desecrated years earlier by Henry VIII. Based on her experiences in England, Mary Ward began to imagine a new type of religious order that would enable English Catholic women

---

* NOTE TO THE READER: There are forty days of Lent, which are counted from Ash Wednesday to sundown on Holy Thursday, excluding Sundays, which always celebrate the Resurrection. These forty days are a time to remember and in some ways emulate the forty days that Jesus Christ spent in the wilderness, fasting and facing temptation. Jesus' forty days in the wilderness echoed the earlier example of Moses, who wandered in the desert for forty years before finding the Promised Land. Noah and his family were also in the ark for forty days during the Great Flood.

to live a consecrated life without attracting the attention of a hostile government.

She founded her new community, the Institute of the Blessed Virgin Mary, primarily for the education of young girls. But Mary broke with convention by permitting her sisters to live outside a convent, to wear lay clothes rather than a religious habit, to travel as necessary, and to govern themselves rather than be governed by the local bishop. These were revolutionary ideas in the seventeenth century, and bishops especially resented the idea that Mary's nuns would be independent of diocesan authority. Thus Mary Ward was imprisoned for heresy on February 7, 1631. She was released on April 14, 1631, on an order from Pope Urban VIII, but papal approval of her new community did not come until 1703, fifty-eight years after her death.

Before she died, Mary Ward, like St. Therese the Little Flower, promised to remember and assist from heaven those she had loved on earth. "When God shall enable me," she told her sisters, "I will serve you."

Hail Mary, daughter of God the Father.
Hail Mary, Mother of God the Son.
Hail Mary, Spouse of God the Holy Ghost.
Hail Mary, Temple of the Most Blessed Trinity.
Hail Mary, Pure Lily of the Trinity, One God.
Hail Mary, Celestial Rose of the love of God.
Hail Mary, Virgin pure and humble, of whom
the King of Heaven willed to be born.
—*Prayer of St. John Eudes*

St. John of Matha

In the twelfth century, the Christians of Spain and Portugal rose up to regain their countries from the Moors who had occupied the land for four hundred years. It was a hard fight, and Christians who fell into Moorish hands generally were taken to North Africa where they were sold as slaves. A French priest born in 1160, John of Matha, wanted to ransom the captives and bring them back to their homes and families, but he had no money for such a huge undertaking. Nonetheless, he collected a band of like-minded men and formed a new religious community—the Order of the Most Holy Trinity and of Captives. They still had no money, so they invoked Mary under the title Our Lady of Good Remedy. Through her intercession donations began to pour in, more than enough for John and his brother Trinitarians to go on their first ransom mission to Morocco.

During John's lifetime he and members of his new religious order traveled into hostile territory, negotiated with unsympathetic officials, and succeeded in ransoming hundreds of Christians.

These missions must have been full of exciting adventures, yet incredibly, the earliest historians of the Trinitarians did not bother to record the details.

The Trinitarians are still in existence, and they are still devoted to Our Lady of Good Remedy. They operate ministries in prisons in over twenty countries around the world, living out the motto they have followed since St. John's day, "*Gloria Tibi Trinitas et captivis libertas*, Glory to you O Trinity and liberty to the captives."

O Lady of Good Remedy, source of unfailing help, grant that we may draw from thy treasury of graces in our time of need. Touch the hearts of sinners, that they may seek reconciliation and forgiveness. Bring comfort to the afflicted and the lonely; help the poor and the hopeless; aid the sick and the suffering. May they be healed in body and strengthened in spirit to endure their sufferings with patient resignation and Christian fortitude.

Don Luis and Our Lady of Ajacan, 1571

After the Spanish established a permanent colony at St. Augustine, Florida, in 1565, Jesuit priests began planning an ambitious missionary campaign along what is now the seaboard of Georgia, the Carolinas, and Virginia. Father Juan Bautista de Segura, vice provincial of the Jesuit community in Havana, Cuba, convinced his superiors to let him open a mission in the territory the Spanish called Ajacan, now known as Stafford County, Virginia. Father de Segura was joined by his fellow priest, Luis de Quiros, three Jesuit lay brothers, Pedro Linares, Gabriel Gomez, and Sancho Zebalics, three Jesuit scholastics or seminarians, Cristobal Rendondo, Baptista Mendez, and Gabriel De Solis, and a servant, Alonso Olmos. Accompanied by a Native American convert named Don Luis, who would act as their interpreter, the missionaries set out for Virginia, landing near the future site of Jamestown in September 1570. They named their mission in honor of Mary—Our Lady of Ajacan.

Right from the start, the mission was in trouble. The missionaries arrived during a severe drought and famine; the crops they planted did not grow, and their only option was to rely on the Indians for food. Then Don Luis abandoned them and returned to his tribe. Unknown to the Jesuits, Don Luis had turned against them and was now inciting his people against the missionaries. A few weeks later he returned to the mission with a large band of Native American warriors; they killed all the Jesuits, looted the mission, and set it on fire. Only Alonso Olmos was spared; he managed to return to Florida where he related what happened at Our Lady of Ajacan.

Father Segura and his companions were men apart: most explorers came to the New World greedy for land and gold, but the missionaries' only ambition was to lead souls to Christ and teach the people of the Americas to love Our Lady.

Thou dost hold my right hand.
Thou dost guide me with thy counsel,
and afterward thou wilt receive me to glory.
Whom have I in heaven but thee?
And there is nothing upon earth that
I desire beside thee.
—Psalm 73:23–25

O n or about this day in 1540, Pope Paul III gave a small church, Santa Maria della Strada, or St. Mary of the Street, to St. Ignatius of Loyola and his fellow Jesuits. The church preserved an ancient icon of the Virgin and Child commissioned around the year 425 by a distinguished Roman family, the Astalli, who had built a small wayside shrine for the holy image.

In 1568 Cardinal Alessandro Farnese, a great supporter of the Jesuits, decided the order deserved something much grander than the small shrine; he had the humble della Strada church torn down and built the spectacular Church of Gesù, or Church of Jesus, on the site. The venerable icon of the Madonna was saved, however, and placed in its own chapel beside the high altar of the new church. Just outside the Madonna's chapel is the tomb of St. Ignatius—which is very appropriate considering how often he said Mass before the icon of Our Lady of the Street.

The Gesù's architect designed an opulent chapel for the painting, with a frescoed dome depicting trumpeting angels, and frescoes of scenes from the life of Mary framed in red marble around the walls. As for the icon itself, golden jewel-encrusted crowns have been superimposed on the images of Jesus and Mary. Such splendor emphasizes St. Ignatius' love for Our Lady, and his complete confidence in her as the patron of the Society of Jesus.

No mother ever had more sons, no one was so blessed or showed more fidelity. None was ever so holy, beautiful, fair, so honored, and endowed with the gifts of the Holy Spirit. No mother ever had more love for her Son.

—*St. Ignatius of Loyola's Meditation on Mary*

Bernadette sees a lady in white in a grotto outside Lourdes, 1858

Fourteen-year-old Bernadette Soubirous was preparing soup on the morning of February 11, 1858, when she discovered that she had no more wood to feed the fire. With her mother's permission, Bernadette, her sister Toinette, and a neighbor girl, Jeanne Abadie, set off for the outskirts of town to collect fallen branches and driftwood along the Gave River. At the grotto of Massabielle, Toinette and Jeanne said they would wade across the river to search for wood on the other side. They pulled off their wooden clogs, gathered up their skirts, and stepped into the water. Immediately, the two girls began to cry because the river water was icy cold. Bernadette, who was wearing woolen stockings, sat down on a rock to remove them before following the other girls.

As she pulled off the first stocking she heard a roaring wind, but observed that the trees along the river did not move. She began to take off her other stocking when the sound of rushing wind came again. She looked up again, and this time a movement in the grotto caught her eye.

When she went over to investigate, she saw a lovely lady dressed in white standing in an oval-shaped fissure in the face of the rock. When the apparition made the sign of the cross, Bernadette did likewise; taking her rosary from her pocket she knelt down and began to pray. That is how Toinette and Jeanne found her, on her knees, her rosary in her hands, her eyes fixed upon the niche in the grotto wall. She appeared to be in some kind of trance, but when she came to her senses Bernadette told the girls she had seen a beautiful lady who had just vanished.

Back home, Toinette repeated Bernadette's story to their mother. At first Louise Soubirous thought her daughters were making up stories, so she beat them with a cane. But when Bernadette insisted that she was telling the truth, her mother became anxious. "We must pray to God," she said. "It is perhaps the soul of one of our relatives in purgatory."

Arise, my love, my fair one, and come away.
O my dove, in the clefts of the rock,
in the covert of the cliff, let me see your face,
let me hear your voice, for your voice is sweet,
and your face is comely.
—*Song of Solomon 2:13–14*

Our Lady returns to Lourdes, 1858

Three days after her first encounter with a mysterious lady at Massabielle, Bernadette Soubirous received her mother's permission to return to the grotto to see if the vision would return. It was Sunday, and after Mass Bernadette walked with two friends to Massabielle; she brought along a bottle of holy water.

At the grotto the three girls knelt and began to pray the Rosary. They had just finished the first decade when Mary appeared. Bernadette sprinkled holy water in the apparition's direction, saying that if the Lady came from God would she please stay, but if she was not from God she must leave them in peace. "She started to smile, and bowed," Bernadette recalled later, "and the more I sprinkled her with holy water, the more she smiled and bowed her head."

Bernadette's friends saw no one, but they all remained at the grotto praying. When they had finished the rosary, Our Lady vanished.

Mary appeared fifteen times more to Bernadette, and with each new vision the crowds that accompanied Bernadette to the grotto increased—particularly after Our Lady showed her where to uncover a spring, and people who had washed themselves with the spring water reported that they had been miraculously healed of a variety of ailments. In the vision on March 25, 1858, the Lady finally identified herself, saying, "I am the Immaculate Conception."

> **In the holy tabernacle**
> **I ministered before him,**
> **and so I was established in Zion.**
> **In the beloved city likewise**
> **he gave me a resting place,**
> **and in Jerusalem was my dominion.**
> **So I took root in an honored people,**
> **in the portion of the Lord,**
> **who is their inheritance.**
> *—Sirach 24:10–12*

Bartolo Longo and Our Lady of the Rosary

One of the most unlikely champions of Our Lady was Bartolo Longo. Although raised in a devout Italian Catholic family that prayed the Rosary together every night, Bartolo became insanely hostile to the Church as a young adult and developed such a hatred for God himself that he joined a satanic cult. His horrified family and friends commenced an intense period of prayer for his sake. At the same time a college professor who knew the Longo family began, very gently, to show Bartolo the absurdity of turning his life over to absolute evil. A Dominican priest helped Bartolo take the next step of full confession and a complete return to the Catholic faith.

To make amends for his years as a satanist, Bartolo became a public speaker against the occult. And since he considered the countless Rosaries offered to heaven for his sake as the cause of his conversion, he became especially devoted to Our Lady of the Rosary, and encouraged others to pray the Rosary frequently. On February 13, 1876 Bartolo watched as workmen began excavations for the Shrine of

Our Lady of the Rosary not far from the ruins of the ancient Roman city of Pompeii. Today the church receives ten thousand pilgrims daily.

In 1926 as he lay dying Bartolo's last words were, "My only desire is to see Mary who saved me and who will save me from the clutches of Satan."

In 1980 Pope John Paul II declared Bartolo Longo "Blessed."

Gate of Heaven, pray for us.
Morning star, pray for us.
Health of the sick, pray for us.
Refuge of sinners, pray for us.
Comforter of the afflicted, pray for us.
Help of Christians, pray for us.
—*From the Litany of the Blessed Virgin*

The first postage stamp bearing an image of Our Lady is printed in Bavaria, 1920

Every Christmas the United States Postal Service issues a stamp depicting the Virgin and Child. Using these lovely stamps on cards and letters at Christmastime is tradition for many people, but the first stamp to bear an image of the Madonna was not produced for a Christmas card but to celebrate a military victory.

In honor of the three-hundredth anniversary of Duke Maximilian I's victory at the battle of White Mountain during the Thirty Years War, the government of Bavaria authorized a new stamp that would depict one the most famous landmarks in Munich—the column bearing a gilded statue of the Blessed Mother that stands in the Marienplatz in front of the city's Cathedral of Our Lady. (Maximilian had erected the statue and column in thanksgiving to Mary, to whose intercession he credited the victory.)

Since that first stamp in 1920 Mary has appeared on hundreds of postage stamps of countries from all over the world. Estonia released the first stamp depicting the Holy Family in 1936. In the 1960s and 1970s, when Bulgaria had a Communist government, the postal service there released a series of stamps depicting icons of the Virgin and Child. And countries that have been historically Catholic, such as Austria, Argentina, Beligium, and the Dominican Republic, have released dozens of Marian stamps over the years. Today, collectors of stamps bearing sacred images can even join a special organization—COROS, Collectors of Religion on Stamps.

My most holy Lady,
I also beseech you to obtain for me
true obedience and true humility of heart
So that I may recognize myself truly
as a sinner—wretched and weak—
and powerless,
without the grace and help of my Creator
and without your holy prayers.
—*St. Thomas Aquinas*

DAY NINE
The bishop of Paris plans a new cathedral for Our Lady, 1160

In the twelfth century virtually every Gothic cathedral built in France was dedicated to Notre Dame, or Our Lady. Of these great churches, the most famous and most recognized is the Cathedral of Notre Dame in Paris. The site of the Cathedral of Notre Dame has been host to a church dedicated to Mary since 537, when the king of the Franks, Childebert, first erected a small church in honor of the Mother of God. By the twelfth century, Childebert's church was in ruinous condition and was too far gone to be repaired. At the same time, the Cathedral of St. Stephen just across the square had taken on a shabby look, so in 1160 Maurice de Sully, bishop of Paris, decided to tear down Childebert's church and the old St. Stephen's and build in their place a cathedral in the new Gothic style. The cathedral would be dedicated to Our Lady of Paris—Notre Dame de Paris and would take 182 years to complete.

Mary's cathedral in Paris became the heart of France's religious and national life. Here kings and queens celebrated their marriages, the birth of their children, and their triumphs over their enemies. St. Louis IX brought the precious relic of Christ's crown of thorns to this church. And here a Church tribunal overturned the condemnation of Joan of Arc, declared her innocent of any wrongdoing, and asserted that she was a true and saintly child of the Catholic faith.

Today approximately fifty thousand visitors tour the cathedral. This foot traffic can be very distracting to anyone who comes to Notre Dame to pray, so the cathedral clergy have created an informal oratory, a quiet corner where the faithful can contemplate a medieval sculpture of Our Lady of Paris and offer up their prayers to the Mother of God.

Hail, Holy Queen, mother of mercy, our life, our sweetness, and our hope.
To thee do we cry, poor banished children of Eve; to thee do we send up our sighs, mourning and weeping in this valley of tears. Turn, then, O most gracious advocate, thine eyes of mercy toward us; and after this our exile, show unto us the blessed fruit of thy womb, Jesus. O clement, O loving, O most sweet Virgin Mary.

Feast of Our Lady of the Thorn

Today we celebrate a metaphor of the Blessed Virgin that was very popular in the Middle Ages when preachers, spiritual writers, and even poets compared Mary to the burning bush through which God spoke to Moses. Just as the bush burned without being consumed, they said, Mary gave birth to Christ without loss of her virginity. In the Office of Lauds for January 1—a date that today is known as the Solemnity of Mary, Mother of God, formerly the Feast of the Circumcision—one of the antiphons prayed, "The bush which Moses saw unburned we recognize as your glorious virginity. Mother of God, intercede for us."

A bit later, the idea developed that the bush was full of thorns—an emblem for sin—but none of them touched Mary, who was conceived without original sin and remained sinless all her life. The medieval English poet Geoffrey Chaucer developed this idea of the burning bush in a prayer to Mary he composed for his "The Prioress's Tale":

O Mother-Maid! O Maiden-Mother free!
O bush unburnt, burning in Moses' sight,
Who ravished so the Soul of Deity,
With thy meekness, the Spirit of the Light,
That his virtue, which was thy soul's delight,
Conceived in thee the Father's wise essence,
Help me to speak now with all reverence!

SECOND SUNDAY OF LENT
The Seven Founders of the Servites

In the first quarter of the thirteenth century when the city of Florence was being torn apart by civil strife, lax morals, and religious controversy, seven young men, all members of the city's well-to-do classes, joined together to consecrate their lives to the pursuit of personal holiness under the protection of the Blessed Virgin in an effort to strengthen their faith. Their names were Buonfiglio dei Monaldi, Giovanni di Buonagiunta, Bartolomeo degli Amidei, Ricovero dei Lippi-Ugguccioni, Benedetto dell' Antella, Gherardino di Sostegno, and Alessio de' Falconieri. Not long after they had organized themselves, Mary appeared before them, accompanied by an angel; Mary held a black monastic habit, while the angel displayed a scroll that read "Servants of Mary." Inspired by the vision, the seven men adopted the black habit and called themselves Servants of Mary—Servites, for short.

The Servites lived an active life, reviving religious devotion among Catholics, convincing heretics to return to the Church, and even traveling as far as Asia as missionaries. At a time when Italy was on the verge of a civil war between supporters of the authority of the pope and supporters of the authority of the Holy Roman Emperor, the Servites acted as arbitrators to restore peace. On several occasions they even risked their lives to break up street brawls and riots.

Pope Leo XIII canonized all seven founders together in 1888. Today there are communities of Servites all across Europe and the Americas, as well as in Australia and South Africa. Their liturgical feast is celebrated on February 17.

May the glorious pleading of the blessed and glorious Mary, ever virgin, shield us, we beseech You, O Lord, and bring us to life everlasting. Through our Lord Jesus Christ Your Son, who lives and reigns with You in the unity of the Holy Spirit, one God, world without end. Amen.

DAY ELEVEN
St. Simeon of Jerusalem,
the last living relative of Jesus and Mary

The second-century historian of the early church St. Hegesippus tells us that St. Simeon was related to Christ; he may have been the son of Clopas and Mary mentioned in St. John 19:25.

After St. James the Lesser, the first bishop of Jerusalem, was martyred in AD 62, the Christians of the city chose Simeon to replace him. About the same time, a revolt against Roman rule broke out in Judea. Initially the rebels were successful in driving out the Roman troops, but Simeon realized Judea had no chance of defeating the Roman Empire. As the Roman legions under the command of Titus marched on the Holy City, Simeon instructed his people to pack their belongings—they were leaving Jerusalem. He led the Jerusalem Christians to the little town of Pella, and there they remained while war raged between the Romans and the Jewish rebels. In 70 the disaster Simeon dreaded befell Jerusalem: it was captured by the Romans, its inhabitants were massacred, any survivors were carried off into slavery, the temple was looted and desecrated, and the city was burned to the ground. Today in Rome, just opposite the Colosseum, stands the Arch of Titus, which shows Roman troops marching into Rome with the spoils of Jerusalem, including the seven-branched menorah from the holy temple.

In 106, when the emperor Trajan began a fresh persecution of the Church, Simeon was still alive. He was arrested, tried, and in spite of his advanced age—Simeon was over one hundred years old—the last living relative of Jesus and Mary was sentenced to be crucified. The Feast of St. Simeon is celebrated on February 18.

He asked life of thee; thou gavest it to him, length of days for ever and ever.
His glory is great through thy help; splendor and majesty thou dost bestow upon him.
Yea, thou dost make him most blessed forever.
—*Psalm 21:4–6*

DAY TWELVE
*Our Lady heals a child and
predicts a victory, 1525*

Antoine, Duke of Lorraine in France, was devoted to the church and to his people—so much so that they called him Antoine the Good. In 1525, when anti-Catholic radicals threatened the peace of his land, Duke Antoine went off to defend it.

Meanwhile, a little girl who had been born unable to hear or speak stopped by the Church of St. George in the town of Nancy to pray at Our Lady's altar. As she prayed she heard a voice—the first sound she had ever heard—instructing her to go to Antoine's wife, the duchess Renee, and tell her that the duke would come home safe and victorious.

The child left the church, called on the duchess, and repeated the voice's message. "Ah!" exclaimed Renee. "That is good news."

The sudden healing of the little girl and the duke's victory over the anti-Catholic radicals brought crowds to Mary's altar in the Church of St. George. More people soon reported miracles. To accommodate the multitude of people who wanted to pray before the statue, it was moved to the cathedral of Nancy, where Mary was given a new title, Our Lady of Good News.

During the French Revolution, when so many sacred images were destroyed, the Catholics of Nancy hid this image of Our Lady. It survives to this day.

Hail Mary, full of grace, the Lord is with thee. Blessed art thou amongst women, and blessed is the fruit of thy womb, Jesus. Holy Mary, Mother of God, pray for us sinners, now and at the hour of our death. Amen.

The shrine to Our Lady in
Boulogne-sur-Mer

During the Middle Ages, the French shrine that held the ancient image of Our Lady of Boulogne-sur-Mer was especially popular with the English royal family. King Henry III and King Edward II, the Black Prince, and John of Gaunt all made the journey across the English Channel to pray before Our Lady of Boulogne-sur-Mer. In the sixteenth century Henry VIII actually stole the statue, setting off a series of intense diplomatic negotiations until he agreed to return the sacred image to the French.

The image is out of the ordinary, and very lovely: it depicts the Virgin and Child standing in a boat, flanked by angels. Tragically, during the French Revolution extremists burned the original and destroyed the church. In 1813 a copy was made, blessed, and installed in a new shrine. In 1938, on the eve of World War II, a few more copies were made and sent on pilgrimage throughout France to increase devotion to the Mother of God.

The shrine suffered another severe blow during World War II when bombs struck the church, damaging the statue beyond repair. Happily, one of the replicas had been safely stored in Lourdes; this statue was brought back to Boulogne in a triumphal procession known as the "Great Return." It is this statue that pilgrims see in the restored church in Boulogne-sur-Mer.

And when they met her they all blessed her with one accord and said to her, "You are the exaltation of Jerusalem, you are the great glory of Israel, you are the great pride of our nation!"
—*Judith 15:9*

DAY FOURTEEN
Forty-eight sailors attribute their deliverance to Our Lady, 1838

In January 1838 a French sailing ship with a crew of forty-eight men set out from Newfoundland on its return voyage to its home port, Paimprol. While they were in the middle of the Atlantic, a terrible storm overtook the ship, battering it for three days. On the third day, waves crashed over the sides of the boat, swamping it. As the ship began to sink, the crew called upon Mary, under her title Star of the Sea, to save them. They promised that if their lives were spared, they would go barefoot in procession to her altar in the parish church when they reached port, and there they would sing the hymn "Ave Maris Stella."

In answer to their prayers the storm faded away and the sea became calm. The crew was able to pump the water out of the hold and repair the sails that had been shredded in the storm. For the rest of the voyage they traveled across a smooth sea.

Once they docked in Paimprol the sailors came ashore barefoot and bareheaded and set off for the church. Their families, who had come to the harbor to greet them, heard the story of the miracle and joined the procession. By the time the sailors reached Our Lady's altar, everyone in town was with them. The entire population of Paimprol knelt before the statue of the Virgin Mary and together sang *Ave Maris Stella*.

Ave Maris stella!,
Dei mater alma,
Atque semper virgo,
Felix caeli porta.

Hail, Star of the Sea!
Dear Mother of God,
Ever-virgin,
And happy gate to Heaven.

DAY FIFTEEN
Blessed James Carvalho
martyred in Japan, 1624

The church's mission to Japan in the sixteenth century had been extremely successful: by 1614 there were between three and four hundred thousand Japanese Catholics in the country. That same year, however, the Japanese government turned against both Europeans and Japanese Catholics. All European missionaries were banished, all churches were closed or destroyed, and all Japanese Catholics were required to make a public declaration denying their faith. In spite of the new legislation, many Japanese Catholics remained faithful, and many missionary priests went into hiding to serve their Japanese parishioners in secret. The result was a wave of intense anti-Catholic persecution in Japan.

Father James Carvalho, a Portuguese Jesuit, had been deported in 1614, but he slipped back into Japan two years later. For eight years he managed to minister to Japan's Catholics and elude the government's priest hunters. But in February 1624 he was discovered and arrested with a dozen Japanese Catholics. They were marched to a river that ran near a prison, stripped, and forced to stand in the icy water while a winter snowstorm raged around them. Father Carvalho led his fellow martyrs in prayers to Our Lord and Our Lady as they froze to death. At the end, when he could barely say a thing, he managed to whisper the names "Jesus" and "Mary."

In 1867 Blessed Pope Pius IX declared James Carvalho "Blessed."

> The LORD is near to all who call upon him,
> to all who call upon him in truth.
> He fulfills the desire of all who fear him, he
> also hears their cry, and saves them.
> The LORD preserves all who love him.
> —*Psalm 145:18–29*

DAY SIXTEEN
Commemoration of the Flight into Egypt

St. Matthew's Gospel (2:13–23) tells how Herod, afraid of the infant the Magi called King of the Jews, plotted to kill the Christ Child. Warned by an angel, Joseph took Mary and Jesus and traveled south to Egypt where they would be beyond Herod's reach. They remained there until the wicked king died and the angel told them it was safe to return home.

The Holy Family's nighttime escape caught the imagination of early Christians, and many legends grew up around their journey. One story says that when Mary and Joseph were hungry a date palm bowed down so they could pick the fruit. Another story tells of statues of pagan gods tumbling off their pedestals and shattering as the Christ Child passed by. The Christians of Egypt have, understandably, an especially rich collection of Flight-into-Egypt folklore, and at one time a host of churches and chapels marked the Holy Family's route through the country.

As is the case throughout the Orthodox world, the Coptic Christians of Egypt turn to the Blessed Virgin in every liturgy and ask for her help and intercession. That Mary, the Christ Child, and St. Joseph once lived in Egypt is a source of great pride for the Copts that intensifies their devotion to the Mother of God, as we can see in this prayer recited during the Coptic liturgy for the Twelfth Hour, what we in the West call Compline:

O Pure Virgin, draw the veil of thy speedy protection upon thy servant. Remove from me the billows of evil thoughts and raise my sick soul to pray and watch, because it has long lain in deep sleep; for thou art able, merciful, helpful, and the Birthgiver of the Spring of Life, my King and my God, Jesus Christ, my hope.

THIRD SUNDAY OF LENT
An epidemic in Rome ends through the intercession of the Blessed Virgin, 591

In a city full of monuments, Rome's Castel Sant' Angelo is one of the most impressive, standing at the foot of the broad boulevard that leads to St. Peter's. The castle was originally the mausoleum of Roman emperor Hadrian. In the Middle Ages it was rebuilt as a fortress to protect the Vatican. Today it is a museum, and from the top of the castle visitors enjoy one of the finest views of the Eternal City.

Towering above the castle is huge bronze statue of St. Michael the Archangel. The statue recalls a legend from the life of Pope St. Gregory the Great. In 591, only a year after Gregory had been elected pope, Rome was devastated by a mysterious epidemic. With the city's doctors powerless to stop the spread of the disease, Pope Gregory turned to the Blessed Virgin for help. Carrying an ancient painting of the Virgin and Child, he led processions through the city, praying that by Mary's intercession God would bring an end to the plague. The procession was crossing the bridge over the Tiber that led to the castle when Gregory had a vision of St. Michael hovering in the sky and sheathing his sword. Gregory understood the vision as a sign that Mary's prayers had been heard, and the epidemic did indeed come to an end.

The painting St. Gregory carried through the streets still survives; today it is enshrined in Rome's Basilica of St. Mary Major, where it is known as Salus Populi Romani, or Protector of the People of Rome, in tribute to the miracle of 591.

> Loving mother of the Redeemer,
> Gate of Heaven, Star of the Sea,
> assist your people who have fallen yet strive to rise again.
> To the wonderment of nature you bore your Creator,
> Yet remained a virgin after as before.
> You who received Gabriel's joyful greeting,
> have pity on us poor sinners.
> —*Alma Redemptoris Mater*

During the seventeenth century, a statue of the Blessed Virgin stood in the chapel of the Ursuline nuns in Perigeuex, France. So many prayers offered before this image were answered that the nuns called it "Our Lady of Great Power." When some of the Perigeuex Ursulines were assigned to a new convent and school in Quebec City, they took a copy of the statue with them and established the Great Power devotion in the New World. One of the sisters became especially devoted to Mary under this title.

About the year 1717, Marie-Jeanne-Madeleine Legardeur de Repentigny joined the Ursulines of Quebec, taking the name Sister St. Agatha. She had been engaged to marry a soldier, a member of the Quebec garrison, but he died before the wedding. Hoping to assuage her grief, Marie entered the convent. At first she found the disciplined life of the Ursulines difficult. To help her persevere in her religious vocation, Sister St. Agatha prayed to Our Lady of Great Power. Soon everything she had found tiresome or unpleasant about convent life faded away. In thanksgiving, Sister St. Agatha promised that she would keep a lamp burning perpetually before the image of Our Lady of Great Power.

After Sister St. Agatha's death, her relatives kept the votive lamp burning before the shrine. This touching token of gratitude to Mary became part of Quebec folklore, known as "the lamp that is never extinguished."

Truly God is good to the upright, to those who are pure in heart. But as for me I nearly stumbled, my steps had well nigh slipped. But for me it is good to be near God; I have made the Lord God my refuge, that I may tell of thy works.
—*Psalm 73:1–2, 28*

St. Denis dedicates a church to Mary, AD 250

Eighteen hundred years ago the Romans erected a temple to Ceres, the goddess of crops and harvests, amid the farmers' fields outside Paris. When St. Denis arrived in Paris around 250 as the city's first bishop, he acquired the temple, consecrated it to Our Lady, and placed an icon of Mary over the altar where the statue of Ceres had once stood. Legend says that this was the first church dedicated to Mary in the diocese of Paris.

One bit of truth in this legend is that St. Denis was indeed the first bishop of Paris. He was so successful at bringing souls into the church that he attracted the attention of Paris's pagan priests; they denounced him to the Roman authorities who sentenced Denis to be beheaded. The site of Denis's martyrdom is known as Montmartre, or the Martyr's Hill. The French built the Basilica of St. Denis over his grave, which became the favorite burial place for the kings and queens of France.

Another part of the story also appears to be accurate: in the Montparnasse neighborhood of

Paris there is a church called Notre Dame des Champs, or Our Lady of the Fields; beneath the church archaeologists have found the remains of a Roman temple. It seems that after the people there were converted to Christianity, the Roman temple was turned into a church named in honor of the Blessed Virgin. It is much harder to pin down whether St. Denis was responsible for the shift from pagan temple to Catholic church.

Nonetheless, with its walls covered in murals depicting twenty-two scenes from the life of the Blessed Virgin, Our Lady of the Fields is indisputably Mary's church.

Thou art the all-honored mother of light. From the rising of the sun to the going down of the same, they offer thee glorification, O Birthgiver of God, the second heaven, for thou art the pure and unchanged blossom and the ever-virgin mother, for the Father has chosen thee and the Holy Spirit overshadowed thee and the Son took flesh from thee. Ask Him to grant salvation to the world which He hast created, and deliver it from temptation. Let us praise Him with a new song and bless Him. Both now and ever and unto the ages of ages. Amen.

—*Prayer to Our Lady from the Coptic Liturgy of the First Hour*

DAY NINETEEN
St. Gabriel Possenti

When St. Gabriel Possenti entered the Passionist order in 1856, he took the name Gabriel of Our Lady of Sorrows. While this name reveals his devotion to Mary, and particularly to her seven sorrows, it is a bit misleading in terms of Gabriel's personality. As a child he was an outgoing, happy boy—in spite of his own sorrows, the death of several of his brothers and sisters, and the loss of his mother when he was only four years old. In adolescence Gabriel was popular with the boys, and liked to flirt with the girls. And at some point he learned how to shoot.

In 1860, while Gabriel was a novice at the Passionists' monastery in Isola di Gran Sasso, a band of rebels from Garibaldi's army rampaged through the town, breaking into homes and shops and setting several buildings on fire. Gabriel arrived on the scene just as one of the soldiers was dragging a screaming woman across the piazza. He rushed the would-be rapist, freed the hysterical woman, and began wrestling with her attacker. Somehow he wrenched a pistol from the man's belt, then, at gunpoint, ordered him out of town.

At that moment the other marauders arrived in the square and burst out in laughter at the sight of one of their own made helpless by a boyish seminarian in a cassock. They were about to make their own move against Gabriel when a lizard darted across the piazza. Gabriel wheeled to the side and shot the lizard through the head. This display of marksmanship dumbfounded the soldiers. Before they could recover, Gabriel ordered them to drop their weapons and get out of town. After this incident, Gabriel of Our Lady of Sorrows became a local hero, and the patron saint of marksmen.

Love Mary! She is loveable, faithful, constant. She will never let herself be outdone in love, but will ever remain supreme. If you are in danger, she will hasten to free you. If you are troubled, she will console you. If you are sick, she will bring you relief. If you are in need, she will help you. She does not look to see what kind of person you have been. She simply comes to a heart that wants to love her. She comes quickly and opens her merciful heart to you, embraces you and consoles and serves you. She will even be at hand to accompany you on the trip to eternity.

—*Meditation of St. Gabriel Possenti*

DAY TWENTY
The International Marian Academy

Franciscan friars founded the International Marian Academy in 1947 as a scholarly organization to study the role of Marian doctrine and devotion in the life of their religious order. They established their headquarters in Rome, and began their work by sponsoring an academic conference on the question of Mary's assumption. In 1947 the Assumption had not yet been defined as a doctrine of the church (the pronouncement from Pope Pius XII would come in 1950).

When he granted the Marian Academy pontifical status in 1961, Pope John XXIII guaranteed that it would be a permanent department or committee within the Vatican administration. The academy is still a scholarly society that uses the best scholarship available for systematic study of the Blessed Virgin's role in the history of redemption, as well as the growth and varieties of devotions to her. "It is our desire," Pope John wrote, "that this our Academy continue, as it has up till now, to work for the friendly union of forces and intent of all other Marian Academies and Societies existing in the world so as to contribute to the praise and honor of the Virgin Mary."

One of the great centers of the study of Our Lady in the United States is the Marian Library/International Marian Research Institute, operated by the Marianist Fathers and Brothers at the University of Dayton in Ohio. The collection includes over 100,000 books, 63,000 articles, and countless other Mary-related materials such as medals, holy cards, stamps, recordings, and over 900 Nativity scenes.

Wisdom is radiant and unfading, and she is easily discerned by those who love her, and is found by those who seek her. She hastens to make herself known to those who desire her. To fix one's thought upon her is perfect understanding, and he who is vigilant on her account will soon be free from care, because she goes about seeking those worthy of her, and she graciously appears to them in their paths, and meets them in every thought.
—Wisdom 6:12–13, 15–16

The Seminarians of the Roman College place their trust in Our Lady of Confidence, 1915

With the outbreak of World War I, Italy drafted its seminarians into the armed forces. Approximately one hundred seminarians from the Roman College, the seminary that today is housed beside the Basilica of St. John Lateran in Rome, were called up. Before going off to war in February 1915, these young men knelt before a painting of the Madonna and Child, the Madonna della Fiducia, or Our Lady of Confidence that was a favorite at the seminary. They believed that through her prayers in the nineteenth century Rome's seminarians had been shielded against two virulent epidemics. Now they asked for her protection in war.

One version of the story tells how all the seminarians except one fell on the battlefield. The survivor collected his comrades' dog tags and had them melted down into a gold and silver frame for Our Lady of Confidence. Another version says that all of the seminarians returned home safely. A third version, and probably the most accurate, says that the seminarians who returned after the Armistice had been signed pooled their resources to have golden crowns made for the Virgin and Child in the painting.

Pope John Paul II, who was deeply attached to the Blessed Mother, did his utmost to encourage seminarians and so visited the Roman College every year. He never left the grounds without praying before Our Lady of Confidence. His successor, Pope Benedict XVI, has continued this custom.

Grant, O Queen of Heaven, that ever in my heart I may have fear and love alike for your most sweet Son. I pray also that, at the end of my life, you, Mother without compare, Gate of Heaven and Advocate of sinners, will protect me with your great piety and mercy, and obtain for me, through the blessed and glorious Passion of your Son and through your own intercession, received in hope, the forgiveness of all my sins. When I die in your love and His love, may you direct me into the way of salvation and blessedness. Amen.

—*From a prayer of St. Thomas Aquinas*

DAY TWENTY-TWO
The first certified miraculous healing occurs in the spring at Lourdes, 1858

Catherine Latapie, thirty-eight years old, lived in the town of Loubajac, about five miles from Lourdes. In October 1856 she fell from a tree and severely injured two fingers of her right hand. The resulting paralysis made it impossible for her to knit, sew, or cook—a serious hardship for a housewife and mother of two children. On an impulse before dawn on March 1, she rose, woke her two children, and set out on foot for the grotto of Massabielle— she was nine months pregnant at the time.

At the grotto she knelt and prayed, then slipped her hand into the spring. Immediately she could move her fingers as well as before the accident. As she gave thanks to God and Our Lady she felt the first labor pangs. She walked the five miles home with her children at her side, and that evening gave birth to a strong healthy boy.

After a thorough investigation, Bertrand-Severe Laurence, Bishop of Tarbes (Lourdes fell within his diocese) declared that Madame

Latapie's fingers had been healed by divine intervention.

That month two other certified healings were recorded at Lourdes. Louis Bouriette, fifty-four years old, had lost the sight in his right eye nineteen years earlier in an accident at the local stone quarry where he worked. Sometime after Madame Latapie's miraculous healing, Bouriette went to the grotto of Massabielle and bathed his blind eye with water from the spring as he prayed to Our Lady. His sight returned immediately.

Blaisette Cazenave, fifty years old, suffered from a chronic, incurable eye infection. She, too, was completely cured after bathing her eyes with water from the Lourdes spring.

O Immaculate Virgin Mary, Mother of Mercy, you are the refuge of sinners, the health of the sick, and the comfort of the afflicted. You know my wants, my troubles, my sufferings. By your appearance at the Grotto of Lourdes you made it a privileged sanctuary where your favors are given to people streaming to it from the whole world.

Over the years countless sufferers have obtained the cure for their infirmities—whether of soul, mind, or body. Therefore I come to you with limitless confidence to implore your motherly intercession. Obtain, O loving Mother, the grant of my requests. Through gratitude for your favors, I will endeavor to imitate your virtues, that I may one day share in your glory. Amen.

—*Novena Prayer to Our Lady of Lourdes*

*Final apparition of Our Lady at Banneux,
Belgium, 1933*

Beginning in January 1933, Mariette Beco experienced a series of visions of the Blessed Virgin in the yard outside her family's house. Mary appeared in the midst of a great light, wearing a sheer white veil and a long white gown tied with a blush sash. Over her right arm she wore a rosary with a golden chain and a golden crucifix, and on her right foot was a golden rose.

Mary's messages to Mariette were simple. She identified herself as the Virgin of the poor, and indicated a stream as a "spring reserved for all nations—to relieve the sick." In her final appearance Our Lady told Mariette, "I am the Mother of the Savior, Mother of God. Pray much." Then she said, "Adieu," and vanished.

From 1935 to 1937, a commission established by the local bishop investigated the supposed visions and messages, and forwarded their report to the Vatican. In 1942 the bishop of Liege approved devotion to Mary under the title the Virgin of the Poor. Approval of the visions themselves came in 1949.

As for Mariette Beco, she stepped out of the limelight, married and raised a family, and never tried to draw attention to herself or profit from what had happened to her.

Chosen daughter of the Father, pray for us.
Mother of Christ the King, pray for us.
Glory of the Holy Spirit, pray for us.
Virgin daughter of Sion, pray for us.
Virgin humble and poor, pray for us.
Virgin gentle and obedient, pray for us.
Handmaid of the Lord, pray for us.
—*From the Litany of Mary, Queen*

At a lonely spot in the forest of Bondy in northern France, three merchants were set upon by robbers who stole all of their valuables and left them tied to trees to die. The three frightened men knew there was little or no chance of any other travelers passing that way, so they turned to Mary for help, praying fervently that she would save them. And she did, sending angels to release the merchants.

In thanksgiving for their miraculous deliverance, the merchants built a small chapel on the spot and told anyone who would listen how Mary had come to their aid. People who lived near the forest began to visit the shrine; soon there were reports of more prayers being answered by Our Lady.

During the French Revolution extremists destroyed the shrine, but it was rebuilt in 1808 and devotion to Mary as Our Lady of the Angels was revived. Today, visitors to the church will see a small ship suspended over the altar, which is a votive offering given by a group of sailors whose lives were spared during a violent storm at sea thanks to the intercession of the Blessed Virgin.

Many nations will come from afar to the name of the Lord God, bearing gifts in their hands, gifts for the king of heaven. Generations of generations will give you joyful praise. Cursed are all who hate you; blessed forever will be all who love you. Rejoice and be glad for the sons of the righteous; for they will be gathered together, and will praise the Lord of the righteous. How blessed are those who love you!
—*Tobit 13:11–14*

DAY TWENTY-FOUR
Giovanni Pierluigi da Palestrina

Giovanni Pierluigi da Palestrina was born on March 4, 1525. The undisputed genius of Catholic liturgical music during the Renaissance, Palestrina's musical life—from his days as a choirboy through his career as a composer and choirmaster—was intimately tied to Our Lady. By age twelve he had been "discovered" and brought from his hometown (Palestrina) about sixty miles from Rome, to sing in the boys' choir in Rome's Basilica of Santa Maria Maggiore, the most important Marian church in Christendom. Years later, from 1561–1566, he was choirmaster at Maria Maggiore. But it is as a composer of church music that Palestrina is most famous.

One story of Palestrina tells of a time during the Council of Trent when the bishops considered outlawing elaborate musical compositions at Mass because the settings often obscured the sacred text. In response, Palestrina composed his "Pope Marcellus Mass" to prove to the Council Fathers that one could have beautiful polyphonic music at Mass and still hear clearly the Latin text of the prayers. It is not certain if this charming story is true; what is certain, however, is that Palestrina's style of composition set a new standard for Catholic church music in which the words of the text could be understood clearly through the soaring, glorious harmonies of the singers. One of Palestrina's greatest supporters and promoters at the time of the Council of Trent was St. Charles Borromeo, who demonstrated just how well suited Palestrina's music was to the reforms of Trent by offering a Solemn High Mass at which the choir sang the "Pope Marcellus Mass" in the presence of the pope. In addition to composing dozens of Masses and motets in honor of Mary, Palestrina set the Magnificat to music no less than thirty-five times.

My soul magnifies the Lord,
and my spirit rejoices in God my Savior,
for he has regarded the low estate of his
handmaiden.
For behold, henceforth all generations
shall call me blessed.
—*Luke 1:46–48*

DAY TWENTY-FIVE
Our Lady of Bonsecours

In 1655 St. Marguerite Bourgeoys, the first schoolteacher in Montreal and the founder of an order of teaching sisters, the Congregation of Notre Dame, urged her fellow colonists to build a chapel in honor of the Blessed Mother. It's said that the governor of the colony, Paul Chomedey de Maisonneuve, chopped down the first oak tree for the construction of the shrine. The chapel was dedicated to Our Lady of Bonsecours, or Our Lady of Good Help, and in 1672, after a visit home to France, St. Marguerite returned to Montreal with a small wooden statue of the Virgin and Child (this statue is still venerated in the church).

Carved over the door of the church is an inscription, "If the love of Mary is graven in your heart, forget not a prayer in passing." Sailors especially responded to that exhortation, making a point of praying in the Bonsecours chapel before a voyage.

In 1982 Pope John Paul II canonized Marguerite Bourgeoys, marking her feast day as March 5. In 2005, on the 350th anniversary of the founding of the chapel, the remains of St. Marguerite were brought to Bonsecours and laid beneath the side altar, right below the statue she had brought to Canada in 1672.

You, who are so deeply and maternally bound to the Church, preceding the whole People of God along the way of faith, hope, and charity, embrace all men who are on the way, pilgrims through temporal life towards eternal destinies, with that love which the Divine Redeemer himself, your Son, poured into your heart from the Cross. Be the Mother of all our earthly lives, even when they become tortuous, in order that we may all find ourselves, in the end, in that large community which your Son called the fold, offering his life for it as the Good Shepherd.

—*From a prayer of Pope John Paul II*

A Miracle of Our Lady of Nazareth, 1182

On a foggy day in 1182 a Portuguese knight, Dom Fuas Roupinho, was out hunting. He sighted a stag, spurred his horse, and gave chase. As the deer vanished into the heavy mist, Dom Fuas's horse galloped faster. Suddenly, the horse reared up on its hind legs, and the knight could see they were teetering on the brink of a cliff. A small cave shrine to the Blessed Virgin, under the title Our Lady of Nazareth, was nearby. Dom Fuas knew the shrine well, and now he called on Mary of Nazareth for help. By Mary's prayer the horse did not plunge over the edge of the precipice. In thanksgiving for his deliverance Dom Fuas built a small memorial chapel on the spot and moved the statue from its cave to the place of honor above the altar.

The chapel Dom Fuas built still stands, although in the eighteenth century the entire interior was covered with the splendid colored tiles that the Portuguese have elevated to an art form. The Portuguese carried devotion to Our Lady of Nazareth to the New World. In Brazil, at Belem do Para, they built a new church to Mary of Nazareth. Today that church receives one million pilgrims every year on the feast day.

> **In the holy tabernacle**
> **I ministered before him,**
> **and so I was established in Zion.**
> **In the beloved city likewise**
> **he gave me a resting place,**
> **and in Jerusalem was my dominion.**
> **So I took root in an honored people,**
> **in the portion of the Lord,**
> **who is their inheritance.**
> *—Sirach 24:10–12*

The holy image of Our Lady of Perpetual
Help arrives in Rome, 1499

According to a sixteenth-century history of the image of Our Lady of Perpetual Help, an Italian merchant traveling through the island of Crete heard of a wonder-working icon of the Virgin and Child. Hoping to harness the power of the icon exclusively for himself, he stole it from the church where it was enshrined. After making a few more sales calls in the Mediterranean he arrived in Rome on March 7 and went to stay at the house of a friend, where he fell deathly ill. Afraid to die with such a sin on his soul, the merchant confessed his crime to a priest and begged his friend to place the icon in a church. The man promised he would, but after the merchant had died the lady of the house declared that she liked the painting and was going to keep it.

At this point in the story Our Lady steps in. In a series of visions, she commanded the husband to keep the promise he made at his friend's deathbed and place the icon in a church. Incredibly, he ignored her. Mary next appeared to the couple's six-year-old daughter, and this time was very specific: she wanted the picture displayed for public veneration in a church between Rome's basilicas of St. Mary Major and St. John Lateran. The little girl repeated to her parents what Mary had told her, and this time, at long last, the couple relented. They gave the sacred image to the only church that fit Our Lady's description, a little place called St. Matthew's. And there it stayed for three hundred years.

When Napoleon conquered Rome in 1789, he concluded that there were too many churches in the Eternal City, and so ordered the destruction of about fifty. Among those scheduled for demolition was St. Matthew's. When the priests who staffed St. Matthew's moved out, they took the image of Our Lady of Perpetual Help with them. For the next sixty-eight years the icon hung in a disused chapel, all but forgotten.

In the mid-nineteenth century the Redemptorists purchased land for a church and novitiate; on their property stood the ruins of St. Matthew's. Among the Redemptorists who came to live there was a priest named Father Michael Marchi. He knew the story of the icon, and, more important, he knew where to find it. With the permission of Blessed Pius IX, the Redemptorists enshrined the image of Our Lady of Perpetual Help to their new church. When he granted the Redemptorists' request, Pope Pius gave them a commission: "Make her known throughout the world." And the Redemptorists have done that ever since.

O Lord Jesus Christ, you have given us your own Mother Mary, whose wonderful image we venerate, to be our Mother ever ready to help us. Grant, we beseech you, that we who continually seek her motherly aid may be found worthy to enjoy unceasingly the fruit of your redemption. You who live and reign with God the Father, in the unity of the Holy Spirit, one God, for ever and ever. Amen.

DAY TWENTY-EIGHT
Our Lady of the Virtues

During the late Middle Ages in France, Portugal, and eventually in Poland, some Catholics began to emphasize the ten virtues of Mary: purity, prudence, humility, fidelity, devotion, obedience, poverty, patience, mercy, and sorrow. Since these traits of Our Lady can be found in the Gospels, particularly in St. Luke, people referred to them as the Evangelical Virtues of the Blessed Virgin. Mary's virtues also gave rise to a new emblem for her—a ten-pointed star.

At the forefront of this new development in praising Mary was St. Jane de Valois (1461–1504), founder of the Order of the Annunciation. St. Jane fashioned a chaplet, or mini-rosary, for her nuns consisting of ten beads, a holy medal of Our Lady, and a crucifix, with instructions to pray a Hail Mary on each bead while meditating on each of Mary's virtues.

In the eighteenth century, a new religious community in Poland, the Marians of the Immaculate Conception, adopted the Ten Virtues devotion and use of St. Jane's chaplet.

From Poland, the practice spread to Lithuania, the Ukraine, and the Czech Republic. Immigrants from these countries brought the Ten Virtues devotion to America. The Feast of Our Lady of the Virtues is celebrated each year on March 8.

> I loved her and sought her from my youth, and I desired to take her for my bride, and I became enamored of her beauty. She glorifies her noble birth by living with God, and the Lord of all loves her. If riches are a desirable possession, what is richer than wisdom who effects all things? And if anyone loves righteousness, her labors are virtues; for she teaches self-control and prudence, justice and courage, nothing in life is more profitable for men than these.
> —*Wisdom 8:2–3, 5–7*

FIFTH SUNDAY OF LENT
St. Catherine of Bologna

O ne Christmas Eve, St. Catherine of Bologna went to the chapel of her convent intending to pray, with all the concentration she could muster, one thousand Hail Marys in honor of the Mother of God. It was midnight when she recited the last Hail Mary. Suddenly, the Blessed Virgin appeared to her bearing the newborn Christ Child, wrapped in swaddling clothes as he had been on the first Christmas.

Catherine was a woman of many gifts. She was skillful painter—some of her works of art have survived to this day. She was a talented baker. She had a gift for management. And she was unfailingly benevolent—so much so that when her community was discussing whether they should reelect her as superior, the only complaint made against Catherine was her tendency to dispense with a rule of the order if it struck her as unkind. She once spent a whole night praying for a notorious criminal who was sentenced to be executed in the morning. By dawn he had repented and died in a state of grace. If one of her nuns overdid her private penances and became ill, Catherine's prayers would restore the sister to health.

Before the beginning of Lent in 1463, Catherine had a premonition of death. She delivered a final conference to her nuns urging them to bear with one another, "enduring with an inexhaustible patience whatever results from differences of temperament."

Catherine died so peacefully that for some time the nuns attending her did not realize she was gone. Her feast is celebrated each year on March 9.

Adorn your bridal-chamber, O Sion, and welcome Christ the King; embrace Mary, who is the gate of heaven, for she brings to you the glorious King of the new light; remaining ever a virgin, yet she bears in her arms the Son begotten before the daystar: Whom Simeon, taking into his arms, declared to the nations to be the Lord of life and death, and Savior of the world.
—Antiphon for the Feast of the Purification of the Blessed Virgin Mary

DAY TWENTY-NINE
Pius VII credits his liberation from captivity to Mary, Help of Christians, 1814

In 1798 Napoleon marched into Rome, seized eighty-one-year-old Pope Pius VI, and dragged the sick man across the Alps as his prisoner. Six weeks after his arrival in France, Pope Pius died. His successor, Pius VII, also had a difficult time with the French emperor.

In 1808 the French were back in Rome, where they tried to frighten Pius VII by aiming cannons at his bedroom window. Napoleon demanded the pope's abdication; Pius refused, and was promptly arrested. For the next six years the emperor kept Pius VII a prisoner, badgering him to surrender papal territory in Italy to him, to approve the bishops he had selected, even to recognize Napoleon's "right" to name bishops in Italy. In 1814, sick, frightened, and isolated from all friends and advisors, Pius signed a draft giving up papal land in Italy. As the draft was not a formal document, it had no legal force; Pius repudiated his surrender within days. Meanwhile, Napoleon's power was crumbling. On March 10 he did not try to stop the pope as he left for Rome. On April 12 Napoleon abdicated.

When Pius arrived at the gates of Rome, thirty young men from Rome's most aristocratic families unharnessed his horses and drew his carriage through cheering throngs all the way to St. Peter's. Pius, weary but happy to be free, attributed his deliverance to the intercession of Mary, Help of Christians.

Most Holy Virgin Mary, Help of Christians,
how sweet it is to come to your feet
imploring your perpetual help.
If earthly mothers cease not to remember
their children,
how can you, the most loving of all mothers
forget me?
Grant then to me, I implore you,
your perpetual help in all my necessities,
in every sorrow, and especially in all my
temptations.
I ask for your unceasing help for all who are
now suffering.
Help the weak, cure the sick, convert sinners.

Grant through your intercessions many
vocations to the religious life.
Obtain for us, O Mary, Help of Christians,
that having invoked you on earth we may love
and eternally thank you in heaven.
—*Prayer of St. John Bosco*

DAY THIRTY
Remembering Jacinta Marto

Jacinta Marto was one of eleven children. Her mother's name was Olimpia, her father's, Emanuelo. Like almost all their neighbors in the village of Fatima, Portugal, the family farmed a few acres and kept a small flock of sheep. The village itself was a collection of one-story stone houses, their exteriors whitewashed or covered with a thin layer of stucco. Beyond the houses lay each family's fields where they grew olives, figs, or grain. Money was always in short supply, but the Martos were proud that they did well enough to keep all eleven of their children in shoes—no Marto child ran about barefoot.

A few houses away lived Jacinta's favorite cousin, Lúcia dos Santos. Although she was three years older than Jacinta, Lúcia played with her cousin everyday. When Lúcia was about eight years old, her parents sent her out to the pasture to watch the sheep; Jacinta was so heartbroken that her cousin didn't come play with her anymore that Olimpia gave the child a few sheep and sent her out to the fields, too, accompanied by her brother Francisco, who was two years older.

Neighbors recalled that Jacinta was a typical little girl. She had a sweet singing voice; she liked to dance; she insisted that her mother arrange her hair every morning because she wanted to look pretty. She was not more or less religious than the other children her age, although one story tells how during Eucharistic processions Jacinta kept her eyes fixed on the Host, certain that at any moment she would be able to see Jesus.

Jacinta Marto, her brother Francisco, and her cousin Lúcia lived such an ordinary peasant life that the world never would have heard of them. Their chance at a quiet life ended in 1917, when they told their parents that while they were out in the pasture with the sheep they had seen the Blessed Virgin. Once a month for the next six months, Mary appeared to the three cousins, giving them a series of messages for the world: to pray the rosary daily for peace, that the pope should consecrate the world to her Immaculate Heart, and to offer up their personal acts of sacrifice and penance for the conversion of sinners. A particular source of fascination are three particular visions, known as the Three Secrets of Fatima, that appeared to the children. The first was a vision of hell; the second was a prediction of World War II. The third vision was not revealed until 2000 when Pope John Paul II authorized the Vatican to publish it; this vision was a prediction of the attempt on John Paul's life in 1981.

> **O my God, I believe, I adore,**
> **I hope, and I love Thee.**
> **I ask pardon for those who do not believe,**
> **do not adore, do not hope,**
> **and do not love Thee.**
> —*Prayer of the Angel of Fatima*

Our Lady of Guadalupe of Estremadura

Catholics in the Americas are familiar with the famous shrine of Our Lady of Guadalupe in Mexico. They are often surprised to learn that there is a Guadalupe shrine in Spain, too. According to the story of the shrine, in the sixth century Pope St. Gregory the Great sent a small wooden statue of the Virgin and Child as a gift to the archbishop of Seville, St. Leander. About two hundred years later, when the Moors conquered Seville, a group of priests took the statue and fled north. For safekeeping, they buried the statue in the province of Estremadura. The statue lay there for another six hundred years, buried and forgotten, until Mary appeared to a Spanish shepherd and instructed him to have priests dig at a spot she indicated. The clergy came with their shovels and uncovered the statue. The priests built a small shrine where local people came to invoke Mary under the title of Our Lady of Guadalupe—because her image had been found near the Guadalupe River.

The shrine and Our Lady acquired a national reputation in 1340 when King Alfonso XI attributed his victory over the Moors at the battle of Rio Salado to the intercession of Our Lady of Guadalupe. In 1389 the Hieronymite monks became custodians of the shrine; they began construction of a large church and monastery, and actively promoted devotion to Mary of Guadalupe.

Christopher Columbus visited the shrine before his voyage to the New World. Several of the most renowned conquistadors—Hernan Cortez, Francisco Pizarro, and Vasco Nunez de Balboa, all native sons of Estremadura—brought devotion to Guadalupe to Spanish America. When Our Lady appeared to St. Juan Diego outside Mexico City in 1531 she asked to be invoked at her new shrine as Our Lady of Guadalupe, thus uniting the old world and the new around her miraculous image.

May the Blessed Virgin Mary and all the saints plead for us with the Lord that we may deserve to be helped and delivered by him who lives and reigns, world without end. Amen.

The site of the first chapel of St. Anne is blessed at Beaupre, Quebec, 1658

The first pilgrimage destination in North America began as a parish church for French settlers at Beaupre, a tiny settlement along the St. Lawrence River. The land for the church was donated by a knight, Sieur Etienne Lessard, and a missionary priest, Father Vignal, who blessed the site and dedicated it to the mother of the Blessed Virgin, St. Anne. Immediately after the blessing, the men of the parish began laying the foundation. One of the parishioners, Louis Guimont, suffered from severe rheumatism, yet by sheer determination he dragged three stones to the building site. After he delivered the third stone to the work crew, he found that his rheumatism was completely cured. This is the first recorded healing at what has become known as the Shrine of St. Anne de Beaupre.

For most of its history the church of St. Anne was a local shrine popular with French Canadian Catholics. In 1670 the first bishop of New France, Blessed Francois de Montmorency Laval, donated a relic of St. Anne to the church.

In 1876 a magnificent new basilica was erected on the site of the old church; the construction attracted a great deal of publicity in Canada and the United States and brought large numbers of pilgrims to the shrine. They have been coming ever since.

Good St. Anne, you were especially favored by God to be the mother of the most holy Virgin Mary, the Mother of our Savior. By your power with your most pure daughter and with her divine son, kindly obtain for us the grace and the favor we now seek. Please secure for us also forgiveness of our past sins, the strength to perform faithfully our daily duties and the help we need to persevere in the love of Jesus and Mary. Amen.

A statue of Our Lady survives iconoclasts, 1568

Chartres has been a center of devotion to Our Lady since the earliest days of the church in France. Beginning in the twelfth century, the people of the town demonstrated their love for Mary by building a glorious cathedral, arguably the loveliest in France, in her name. The cathedral is a treasure house of fine works of art, but best of all are its stained glass windows. Since this is Mary's church, the dominant color chosen by the medieval craftsmen is blue, and a luminous blue it is, unlike anything seen in stained glass before or since. The hue—known as Chartres blue—has never been replicated.

During the Reformation, when France was torn apart by a tragic civil war between Catholics and Protestants, Chartres became a target of Huguenot iconoclasts who had already desecrated countless churches, burning holy relics, destroying sacred images, and reducing stained glass windows to splinters. When a Huguenot army arrived outside the walls of Chartres, the garrison dug in for a hard fight.

Over one of the city gates stood a statue of the Blessed Mother. As if to demonstrate what they had in mind, the Huguenots aimed their muskets and cannons at the statue with the intention of blasting it apart. But not a single musket ball or cannon shell struck the image of Mary—although the battlements all around it were heavily damaged. In the end, the Huguenots did not capture Chartres, and the intact statue of Mary was moved to a chapel, where the area around her shrine was decorated with the cannonballs that had not touched her image.

O Holy Virgin, who, entering the heavenly mansions, filled the angels with joy and man with hope, vouchsafe to intercede for us at the hour of our death, that, being delivered from the temptations of the devil, we may joyfully pass out of this world to enjoy the happiness of eternal life. Amen.

DAY THIRTY-FOUR
St. Longinus, who pierced the side of Our Lord

At the foot of the cross with Mary and St. John and St. Mary Magdalene were other less sympathetic witnesses to Christ's death, namely the Roman soldiers in charge of the crucifixion. St. John's Gospel tells us that one of these soldiers, to ensure that Jesus was dead, "pierced his side with a spear, and at once there came out blood and water" (Jn. 19:34). St. Matthew's Gospel records that at the moment of Christ's death, as Calvary was shaken by an earthquake, a Roman centurion exclaimed, "Truly this was the Son of God!" (Mt. 27:54).

Tradition has assumed that the Roman who pierced Our Lord's side with a lance also made the dramatic confession of faith. By the year 300, Christians had given the soldier a name— Longinus. He was soon venerated as a saint, and other legends grew up around him: that he had suffered from an eye ailment that was cured when drops of Christ's blood splashed onto his eyes; and that he died a martyr in Cappadocia, in modern-day Turkey.

Both the Catholic and the Orthodox churches honor his memory each year on March 15. The Basilica of the Holy Sepulcher in Jerusalem houses a chapel of St. Longinus, and in St. Peter's in Rome a giant statue of St. Longinus guards the high altar.

O Mother of Sorrows, for the love of this Son, accept me for thy servant, and pray to him for me. And Thou my Redeemer, since Thou hast died for me, permit me to love Thee, for I wish Thee and nothing more.

The Martyrdom of St. John de Brebeuf, 1649

St. John de Brebeuf is famous as the most intrepid and successful of the Jesuit missionaries to the Hurons in New France. Less well known are his mystical experiences, most of which were Mary-related. While praying the Litany of the Blessed Virgin he had a vision of terrifying creatures who appeared intent on harming him; on another occasion Jesus and Mary appeared to him, although neither spoke; once he saw a great crowd of women saints and enthroned above them all the Blessed Virgin; finally, he saw his brother Jesuits wearing blood-red cassocks, which he took as a sign that many of the missionaries, himself included, would die as martyrs.

In late winter 1649 St. John and his fellow Jesuit, St. Gabriel Lalemant, were visiting a string of Huron missions near Georgian Bay in what is now the province of Ontario. The two priests were spending the night at the Mission of St. Louis when the Iroquois made a surprise attack. Startled out of their sleep, the Huron warriors put up a desperate defense so at least some of the women and children could escape, but the Iroquois overwhelmed them. Among the captives were the two French priests. The sufferings of these missionaries are too gruesome to repeat. St. John died after about seven hours of torture; St. Gabriel survived for almost twelve hours.

When word reached the Iroquois that a force of French settlers and Hurons from surrounding missions was on its way, they ran into the forest, leaving the bodies of the martyrs where they lay. The French and Native American rescue party carried the bodies of the martyrs back to the Mission of St. Marie-among-the-Hurons for burial. Today, the relics of St. John and St. Gabriel are venerated in the Church of the Martyrs in Midland, Ontario.

Queen of angels, pray for us.
Queen of patriarchs, pray for us.
Queen of prophets, pray for us.
Queen of apostles, pray for us.
Queen of martyrs, pray for us.
—*From the Litany of the Blessed Virgin*

St. Joseph of Arimathea

The church had barely emerged from the catacombs when Christians began speculating about the extended family of Jesus, Mary, and Joseph. During the second century Christians spoke confidently of Mary's parents, St. Anne and St. Joachim. In succeeding centuries more individuals were added to Christ's family tree until, by the eve of the Reformation, the Holy Family was surrounded by a throng of aunts, uncles, and cousins. One of the legends about the Holy Family claimed that St. Joseph of Arimathea was Mary's uncle. As a wealthy merchant, his business took him to the far corners of the Roman Empire. On a business trip to Britain, it was said, he took along his great-nephew, the child Jesus. Centuries later the eighteenth-century English poet William Blake immortalized this legend is his poem "Jerusalem":

> And did those feet in ancient time
> Walk on England's mountains green?
> And was the holy Lamb of God
> On England's pleasant pastures seen?

The few facts we possess about St. Joseph come from the four Gospels, all of which describe him as a wealthy man, a secret disciple of Our Lord, who on that dreadful Friday found the courage to go to Pontius Pilate and request the body of Jesus. Along with Nicodemus, another furtive disciple, Joseph took Christ's body down from the cross, wrapped it in linen, and carried it to a cave tomb he had prepared for his own use. From the moment the stone was rolled across the entrance of the tomb, Joseph of Arimathea disappeared from the historical record.

At this point, the King Arthur legend steps in, asserting that Joseph stood at the foot of the cross and caught the Lord's blood in the cup Christ had used at the Last Supper—the Holy Grail. Years later Joseph carried his relics of the Precious Blood and the Grail to England, to the site of modern-day Glastonbury, where he enshrined them. No one has ever found St. Joseph's relics, but archaeologists have discovered at Glastonbury traces of what may have been a chapel built during the early years of Christianity.

O God, by whose grace St. Joseph of Arimathea was emboldened to ask for the sacred Body of our Lord Jesus Christ, that together with St. Nicodemus he might prepare it for burial and lay it in his own tomb, give us such an increase of faith and courage that we may not fear to bear reproach for the sake of Christ, but rather may serve him with sincere devotion all the days of our life. Through the same our Lord Jesus Christ, your Son, who lives and reigns with you in the unity of the Holy Spirit, God, forever and ever.

Our Lady of Mercy calls for penance, 1536

In 1223 St. Peter Nolasco, St. Raymond of Penafort, and King Peter of Aragon agreed to found a religious community of men dedicated to ransoming Christian slaves and prisoners of war in North Africa. It is said Mary appeared to these men to bless their efforts and to promise that this new religious order would always be under her protection. After the vision, the two saints and the king invoked Mary as Our Lady of Mercy, and called the members of the new order "Mercedarians," from *merced,* the Spanish word for mercy. Since then, Mary, the Mother of Mercy, has been one of the most appealing titles of Our Lady.

On March 18, 1536, an Italian laborer from the town of Savona, Antonio Botta, was on his way to a job when the Virgin Mary appeared before him. He listened, astonished and frightened, as she gave him a message for everyone in Savona. In reparation for their sins and in her honor, Mary called upon them all to fast for three successive Saturdays. When she had finished delivering her message, Mary raised her hands, looked up to heaven, and repeated three times, "Mercy, not justice, my Son."

Antonio spread the word, and the people fasted as Mary instructed. No disaster or any other sign of God's displeasure afflicted their town, so they believed that their acts of penance had been accepted in heaven. In gratitude to the Blessed Mother who had pleaded with Christ on their behalf, the townspeople acclaimed Mary as their patron under the title Our Lady of Mercy of Savona.

Holy Mary, help the miserable, strengthen the discouraged, comfort the sorrowful, pray for your people, plead for the clergy, intercede for all women consecrated to God. May all who venerate you feel now your help and protection. Be ready to help us when we pray, and bring back to us the answers to our prayers. Make it your continual concern to pray for the people of God, for you were blessed by God and were made worthy to bear the Redeemer of the world, who lives and reigns forever. Amen.

—*From a prayer to Our Lady of Mercy*

Devotion to St. Joseph, her husband

S t. Joseph, the husband of Mary and foster
father of Jesus, has become such an essential
part of Catholic religious life that it is incredible
to recall that for the first fourteen hundred years
of the church's existence there was almost no
devotion to him at all. Blame it on the host of
Christological heresies that plagued the early
church: so many saints, popes, and theologians
were occupied with asserting that Jesus Christ
is truly the Son of God, the Second Person of
the Blessed Trinity, that it must have seemed
counter-productive to encourage devotion to the
man who most certainly was not Christ's father.

By the 1400s, however, a small devotion to
St. Joseph was developing in Western Europe.
This devotion got fresh impetus in 1479 when
Pope Sixtus IV added a feast of St. Joseph to the
church's liturgical calendar (March 19). From
that moment, love for St. Joseph grew at an
explosive rate. St. Teresa of Ávila regarded him
as her personal champion and named almost
all of her reformed Carmelite convents in St.
Joseph's honor. The Jesuits carried devotion to

him across Europe and to mission territory in Asia and the Americas.

As if to make up for lost time, the faithful, and even the popes, heaped fresh honors on St. Joseph: because he was the husband of Mary, he was named guardian of virgins; because he loved, protected, and supported Jesus and Mary, he was named patron of families; because Jesus and Mary had been with him at the moment of his death, he was named patron of the dying and of a happy death. He became patron of the New World, of the missions in China, of the universal church, and of all who fight against Communism. St. Joseph, once ignored, has become for the church what he was for Mary and Jesus—the indispensable man.

St. Joseph, son of David, and husband of Mary! We honor you, guardian of the Redeemer, and we adore the Child you named Jesus. St. Joseph, patron of the universal Church, pray with us that we may imitate you in lifelong dedication to the will of the Savior.
—*Novena Prayer to St. Joseph*

St. Peter Julian Eymard introduces a new title for Mary

Love for the Blessed Virgin and devotion to the Blessed Sacrament lay at the heart of St. Peter Julian Eymard's religious life. After five years as a diocesan priest he joined the Marists. While praying at the shrine of Our Lady of Fourvieres, St. Peter Julian had an inspiration. "One idea haunted me," he recalled later. "Jesus in the Blessed Sacrament has no religious institute to glorify his mystery of love…. I promised Mary to devote myself to this end."

With the encouragement of the archbishop of Paris and the approval of Blessed Pope Pius IX, in 1857 St. Peter Julian founded his congregation of Blessed Sacrament Fathers in Paris. The priests of his new order focused on two things: regular parish work and perpetual adoration of the Blessed Sacrament exposed in their chapel.

When he formally resigned from the Marists in order to participate fully in his new congregation, some critics accused Peter Julian of being inconstant in his religious vocation.

He excused these detractors and never spoke ill of them. And, of course, he never lost his love for Mary. During the last retreat he gave to the Blessed Sacrament Fathers he suggested that they promote devotion to Mary under a new title—Our Lady of the Blessed Sacrament.

To love Jesus, to live for Jesus, to suffer for Him, to make Him known and loved by all hearts, to consecrate to Him every motion of her own heart, that was Mary's whole desire.

—*A meditation of St. Peter Julian Eymard*

Devotion to Our Lady of Sorrows

"Standing by the cross of Jesus were his mother, and his mother's sister, Mary the wife of Clopas, and Mary Magdalene." (Jn. 19:25)

"A sword will pierce through your own soul also." (Lk. 2:35)

Devotion to Mary as the Sorrowful Mother is based on these two lines from the Gospels—St. John's description of the people who stood at the foot of Christ's cross and Simeon's prophecy to Mary on the day the infant Jesus was presented in the temple. Many moments in Mary's life—the mystery of her Immaculate Conception, her glorious assumption into heaven—fill us with awe, but her grief as she stood at the foot of the cross and watched her son die touches our hearts. All of us who have known sorrow can draw especially close to Mary on this day of all days. And in the Sorrowful Mother we find a friend and intercessor ready to console us and help us bear our own troubles.

Our Lady was first invoked as the Mother of Sorrows during the Middle Ages when St. Francis of Assisi, St. Bridget of Sweden, and many other saints placed renewed emphasis on the close human bond that existed between Mary and Jesus. Artists responded by introducing a new image of the Virgin and Child—the Pieta, in which a grief-stricken Mary cradles the body of Jesus, just taken down from the cross. The human bond between Mary and Jesus also inspired a new hymn, "Stabat Mater," sung to this day at Stations of the Cross.

At the Cross her station keeping,
stood the mournful Mother weeping,
close to Jesus to the last.
Through her heart, His sorrow sharing,
all His bitter anguish bearing,
now at length the sword has passed.
Is there one who would not weep,
whelmed in miseries so deep,
Christ's dear Mother to behold?

*Rose Hawthorne Lathrop asks Mary for help
with her new community, 1898*

On Holy Saturday, when the memory of Christ's sufferings is balanced by expectation of his Resurrection, it is well to recall an American woman who lived most of her life between Good Friday and Easter. She was one of America's most unexpected converts to the Catholic faith, and her name was Rose Hawthorne Lathrop, the daughter of author Nathaniel Hawthorne, descended from a long line of staunch Puritans. She entered the church in 1891 and immediately immersed herself in the rituals of Catholic devotional life—near-daily attendance at Mass with frequent reception of Holy Communion; pausing throughout the day and night to invoke favorite saints; making novenas for the sake of her spiritual and temporal needs. If Rose's diary is any indication, her novena prayers were almost always answered in the affirmative.

Rose had a compassionate heart, and the tragic story of a poor seamstress who died miserably of cancer in the Hospital for Incurables on New

York City's Blackwell's Island gave her an idea that would change her life. She trained as a cancer nurse and then rented a loft and turned it into a free hospital for cancer patients with no financial resources and no one to care for them. Several women volunteered to help, but some of them proved to be quirky and even distinctly odd, which made Rose's patients more uncomfortable. She longed for a community of dedicated women who would do everything possible to make the sick and the dying comfortable, while helping them prepare spiritually for their passage into the next world.

With the Feast of the Annunciation three days away, Rose began a Triduum in honor of the Blessed Mother, begging her to send helpers who were capable of "perfect service," as she put it, to the sick poor. In 1900 Rose formally founded a religious community to nurse indigent, incurable cancer patients, known today as the Dominican Sisters of Hawthorne.

Most holy and immaculate Mary, since Almighty God has preserved you from all stain of sin in order that you might be a worthy Mother for your only Son, who

took on human flesh and became man in your womb, I beseech you, most pure and blessed of all women, to obtain for me complete pardon for all my sins so that I may merit in this life the eternity which I seek. This I ask through your Son who lives and reigns through all ages, world without end. Amen.

—*Novena prayer attributed to Blessed Junípero Serra*

Entering the tomb, they saw a young man sitting on the right side, dressed in a white robe; and they were amazed. And he said to them, "Do not be amazed; you seek Jesus of Nazareth, who was crucified. He has risen, he is not here."

(Mk. 16:5–6)

"Shine! Shine, O new Jerusalem, for the glory of the Lord hath shone on thee. Rejoice and exult, O Sion! And thou, O pure Mother of God, be glad for the Resurrection of thy Son."

(from the Byzantine liturgy for Easter)

E aster was the first holy day celebrated by the church, but the date on which this greatest of all feast days was kept varied from place to place. Centuries passed before there was any uniformity on the subject, and even today the Western and the Eastern Churches differ. (The problem is the choice of calendar: Catholic and Protestant churches follow the calendar that was reformed by Pope Gregory XIII in 1582, while many Orthodox Churches follow the calendar established by Julius Caesar in 46 BC.)

A long-standing tradition asserts that the first person to whom the risen Jesus appeared was his Blessed Mother. During the fifteenth century, this appearance of Christ was a popular subject with artists in northern Europe. The scene usually showed Mary dressed in black or very dark blue, with tears on her cheeks but an expression of surprised joy upon her face as her Son suddenly enters the room.

The Gospels do not record this moment, just as they do not record the names of Mary's parents, the wedding of Mary and Joseph, or the death of St. Joseph. According to the Gospels, the first person to see Jesus in his resurrected glory was St. Mary Magdalene, but tradition has assumed that before he appeared to the Magdalene, Jesus showed himself to another Mary who was much more dear to him.

> Queen of heaven rejoice, alleluia,
> For he whom you did merit to bear, alleluia,
> Has risen, as he said, alleluia;
> Pray for us to God, alleluia.
> Rejoice and be glad, O Virgin Mary, alleluia.
> For the Lord has indeed risen, alleluia.

THE EASTER SEASON*
Pope Benedict XV declares Our Lady of Loreto patron of all aviators, 1920

The Shrine of Our Lady of Loreto in Italy does not attract the enormous crowds that gather at Lourdes, Fatima, and Guadalupe in Mexico. Nonetheless, in the last six hundred years at least fifty popes have made the pilgrimage to Loreto; Pope John Paul II came three times during his twenty-six-year pontificate.

The shrine's origins are mysterious. Legend says that after Muslim forces drove the last of the crusaders from the Holy Land in 1291, angels descended from heaven, lifted the house of the Holy Family in Nazareth off its foundation, and carried it to Loreto, Italy, where it would be safe from any desecration. It is certain that Our Lady was venerated in a shrine at Loreto by 1472. In succeeding centuries the little stone house said to have been the home of Jesus, Mary, and Joseph was encased in marble and became the centerpiece of a magnificent basilica.

In 1920, just seventeen years after the Wright brothers made the first manned air flight, and

NOTE TO THE READER: There are fifty days of Easter, ending at Pentecost.

as aviation clearly was becoming the travel technology of the future, Pope Benedict XV officially declared Our Lady of Loreto patron of aviators, a patronage which Catholics in the aviation industry have extended to pilots, passengers, and flight attendants.

> **Mystical rose, pray for us.**
> **Tower of David, pray for us.**
> **Tower of ivory, pray for us.**
> **House of gold, pray for us.**
> **Ark of the covenant, pray for us.**
> **Gate of heaven, pray for us.**
> —*From the Litany of Loreto*

DAY THREE
English Catholic colonists land in Maryland, 1634

Life for Catholics in seventeenth-century England was difficult, almost impossible. The law forbade them to attend Mass, to receive the sacraments, even to let a priest step across the threshold of their homes. When the noble Calvert family converted to Catholicism, they used their influence with King Charles I to lobby for a colony in the New World where English Catholics could practice their faith freely. The king acquiesced, and named the colony Maryland after his French Catholic wife, Queen Henrietta Maria. No doubt the colonists thought of their new home as dedicated to the Queen of Heaven.

On the Feast of the Annunciation about 140 English Catholic colonists came ashore at St. Clement's Island, Maryland. There Father Andrew White, sj, celebrated Mass in the New World for the first time. Armed with a charter from King Charles I, the Catholics were guaranteed a colony where they could practice their religion freely—something denied them back home in England.

Father White left a brief account of the day. "On the day of the Annunciation of the most Blessed Virgin Mary," he wrote, "we celebrated Mass for the first time in this island: this has never been done before in this region of the world."

After Mass had been said, several men of the new colony fashioned an enormous cross from two logs. With Governor Leonard Calvert lending a hand, they erected it "In honor of Christ our Savior." Then everyone knelt and prayed the Litany of the Holy Cross.

My soul magnifies the Lord,
and my spirit rejoices in God my Savior,
for he has regarded the low estate of his
handmaiden.
For behold, henceforth all generations shall
call me blessed;
for he who is mighty has done great things
for me,
and holy is his name.

And his mercy is on those who fear him
from generation to generation.
He has shown strength with his arm,
he has scattered the proud in the
imagination of their hearts,
he has put down the mighty from their thrones,
and exalted those of low degree;
he has filled the hungry with good things,
and the rich he has sent empty away.
He has helped his servant Israel,
in remembrance of his mercy,
as he spoke to our fathers,
to Abraham and to his posterity forever.
—*Luke 1:46–55*

DAY FOUR
St. Gabriel the Archangel

In the Byzantine Catholic and Eastern Orthodox Churches March 26 is the annual feast of the archangel who first said the words, "Hail Mary." St. Luke's Gospel tells us that before God sent him to Mary, Gabriel appeared to the elderly priest Zachary to tell him that his wife, Elizabeth, would bear a son—the future St. John the Baptist. But it is Gabriel's second annunciation that is most famous—and rightly so, since it announced the coming of the Savior, Jesus Christ. The angel's greeting to the Virgin is repeated by millions every day: "Hail Mary, full of grace, the Lord is with thee."

Generations of Catholics have assumed that Gabriel is the unnamed angel who reassured St. Joseph and urged him to take Mary as his wife, who announced the birth of Christ to the shepherds outside Bethlehem, who warned the Magi not to return to Herod, and who commanded Joseph to get up at once and take Jesus and Mary to Egypt. Some also believe that Gabriel consoled Christ during his agony in the Garden of Gethsemane, and that on the last day Gabriel will blow a trumpet to make one final annunciation—that time itself has come to an end.

Because of his role in the Annunciation, Gabriel has been taken as the patron saint of messengers, postal workers, broadcasters, and anyone else who bears messages or brings news. In the Roman Catholic Church St. Gabriel's feast day is celebrated on September 29 with the two other archangels, St. Michael and St. Raphael.

And so it was that not merely an angel but the archangel Gabriel was sent to the Virgin Mary. It was only fitting that the highest angel should come to announce the greatest of all messages.... So too Gabriel, who is called God's strength, was sent to Mary. He came to announce the One who appeared as a humble man to quell the cosmic powers. Thus God's strength announced the coming of the Lord of the heavenly powers, mighty in battle.

—From a homily by Pope Saint Gregory the Great

DAY FIVE
Ireland's Industrial Rosary Crusade

In 1950, Irish Dominicans, led by Father Gabriel M. Harty, OP, of Dublin, fanned out across their country to encourage working people to make praying the rosary part of their workday. This movement began with Pope Pius XII's call for a revival of religious life in observance of the Holy Year. The Industrial Rosary Crusade was the Dominicans' ambitious and unconventional answer to the pope's appeal.

Each group, or cell, of the movement was founded by the workers themselves, as long as they had the approval of management. At some point during the day members came together to pray the rosary—the exact time for their prayers was another point decided in discussions with their supervisors.

In his travels around Ireland, Father Harty found that workers had established cells on the docks, in railway yards, in chocolate factories, even in Dublin's elegant Customs House. In many places they had set up small shrines in their workplace, used as inspiration throughout the day and as a place to gather when they prayed the rosary. Some places even sponsored May Crownings.

O Mary, Queen of the Universe, we your subjects come before you, and in union with your servant Dominic, stretch forth our hands to receive the gift of your Holy Rosary. Fill our minds with understanding and our hearts with love of the mysteries which we contemplate.
—*From the Industrial Rosary Crusade prayer*

Pope St. Sixtus III and the Basilica of St. Mary Major

P ope St. Sixtus, a Roman priest and a friend and correspondent of the great St. Augustine, was elected to the papcy in 432, one year after the Council of Ephesus, which declared that since Jesus Christ is both true God and true man, it is entirely fitting to address the Virgin Mary as Mother of God. To celebrate this affirmation of Mary's unique role in the salvation of the world, Pope St. Sixtus launched a reconstruction and decoration program at Basilica di Santa Maria Maggiore, or the Basilica of St. Mary Major, the most important church in Rome dedicated to Our Lady.

The previous church, constructed about a century earlier, had become dilapidated. The church Pope Sixtus commissioned surpassed the old one in every respect. It was longer, higher, and more opulently decorated. Over the last sixteen hundred years Pope Sixtus's church has been embellished and expanded in ways that he could never have predicted, but the core of St. Mary Major has barely changed since the fifth century. For example, the beautiful colored marble columns Sixtus had collected from ancient Roman buildings still support the ceiling. But the most significant and longest-lasting of Sixtus's contributions to the decor of St. Mary's is the cycle of mosaics that depict stories from the Old Testament and the life of Mary. Pilgrims to the basilica can also see relics of the manger of Bethlehem below the high altar; the tombs of St. Jerome, the great biblical scholar, and St. Pius V, the pope of the Counter-Reformation; as well as a beautiful white marble sculpture of Mary, Queen of Peace, installed by Pope Benedict XV at the end of World War I.

The inspiration for these works of art was not pride or connoisseurship, but a pope's desire to show his reverence for the Mother of God. The feast of Pope St. Sixtus III is celebrated each year on March 28.

Dearest Mother Mary, drawn to you by your goodness, sympathy, and motherliness, and also because of my needs, I come before you today. I love you, dearest Mother, and I pray that I may learn to love you more and

more. I ask you to keep me always under your special protection, and to help me in all my needs especially for [mention your request here]. Please listen with love to the prayers and petitions of all who come to your shrine to seek your aid and to honor you. Also, obtain for each one of us through your powerful intercession with Jesus, your Son, all the graces we need to lead good lives and follow his teachings, especially his command to love one another. Amen.

—*Novena prayer to Our Lady of Monte Cassino*

DAY SEVEN
Our Lady of the Pillar heals a young Spanish peasant, 1640

In about AD 40 the apostle St. James traveled to Spain to preach the gospel. He settled in the town of Saragossa, but he had little success converting the inhabitants. One day when he was especially depressed about the failure of his mission, the Blessed Virgin appeared to him. To console him, she gave James a small wooden statue of herself bearing the Christ Child in her arms, and a small jasper pillar on which to display the statue. Today the statue, known as Our Lady of the Pillar, is enshrined in a magnificent baroque basilica in Saragossa.

In July 1637 a twenty-year-old Spanish peasant, Miguel Juan Pellicer, had filled a farm cart with grain and was riding the cart mule back to his family's farm when he fell off; one of the cart wheels rolled over his leg, crushing it. Miguel was taken to a hospital, but gangrene set in and the surgeons had no choice but to amputate his leg. Rendered virtually useless on his family's farm, Miguel resorted to begging. Despite these dire circumstances, the young man, who had always been devoted to Our Lady of the Pillar, implored Mary every day to help him at least support himself.

On the night of March 29, 1640, Mary answered Miguel's prayer in an unexpected manner while he slept—she restored his lost leg. Miguel's mother was the first to discover the miracle; when she looked in on her sleeping son before she went to bed, she saw two feet sticking out from the edge of the blanket instead of one. Both the state and the church investigated the case; a year later the archbishop of Saragossa delivered their decision: the healing of Miguel Jan Pellicer was "wonderful and miraculous."

Holy Mary, help the helpless, strengthen the faithful, comfort the sorrowful, pray for the people, plead for the clergy, intercede for all women consecrated to God; may all who keep thy sacred commemoration experience the might of thine assurance.
—*Prayer of Blessed Pope John XXIII*

Blessed Maria Restituta Kafka

Helena Kafka was the daughter of a Czech shoemaker who moved his family to Vienna in 1896, when Helena was only two years old. While in her teens, Helena took a hospital job as a nurse's assistant; she had already thought of the religious life, and now decided to join a nursing order.

In 1913 she joined the Franciscan Sisters of Christian Charity who worked in the Moedling Hospital about twenty miles south of Vienna. In the convent, Helena took a new name—Maria, in honor of Our Lady, and Restituta, in honor of an obscure Roman martyr who gave her life for the faith in 272. Sister Maria Restituta proved to be a gifted nurse; after her superiors arranged for her to be trained in surgery, she became the hospital's chief surgical nurse.

Austria was a Catholic country, yet after the Anschluss of 1938 when Hitler absorbed Austria into the Third Reich, many public expressions of Catholicism were banned. About the same time, the Moedling Hospital had erected a new wing and Sister Maria Restituta had personally hung crucifixes in every room—a traditional practice in Catholic hospitals all over the world. Under the Nazis, crucifixes in hospitals were not permitted; the Moedling staff was ordered to take the crosses down. But Maria Restituta retrieved the crucifixes and hung them up again. Like Our Lady, she would not be kept away from the foot of the cross.

A doctor at the hospital denounced her to the Nazis. On Ash Wednesday, 1942, the Gestapo arrested Sister Maria Restituta as she emerged from the operating room. In October she was found guilty of "favoring the enemy and conspiracy to commit high treason"; for this crime the court sentenced her to death. She spent another five months in prison until she was taken from her cell and decapitated.

In 1998, during a visit to Vienna, Pope John Paul II declared Sister Maria Restituta "Blessed." Her feast is celebrated on March 30.

Let thy steadfast love come to me, O LORD, thy salvation according to thy promise; then shall I have answer for those who taunt me, for I trust in thy word. I will keep thy law continually, for ever and ever; and I shall walk at liberty, for I have loved thy precepts. I will also speak of thy testimonies before kings, and shall not be put to shame; for I find my delight in thy commandments, which I love.

—Psalm 119:41–42, 44–47

Knute Rockne is most famous as Notre Dame's innovative, charismatic football coach. He introduced the forward pass and the shift formation to his players, and even designed some of his own equipment to increase his players' speed on the field without jeopardizing their safety. In his thirteen years as head coach (1918–1930) Rockne racked up an incredible record: 105 wins, 12 losses, 5 ties, and 6 national championships.

Less well known is that while coaching at Notre Dame, Rockne, a Lutheran from Norway, converted to Catholicism. He had long been devoted to Notre Dame the school, but he became devoted to the person of Our Lady, too.

On March 31, 1931, while on a flight to Los Angeles, a wing snapped off Rockne's aircraft. The plane crashed into a wheat field in Bazaar, Kansas, killing everyone onboard. In his eulogy at Rockne's funeral in Notre Dame's chapel, the university's president, Father Charles O'Donnell, csc, praised Rockne's devotion to Our Lady. "He might have gone to any university in the land

and been gladly received and forever cherished there. But he chose Our Lady's school, Notre Dame. He honored her in his life as a student, he honored her in the monogram he earned and wore, he honored her in the principles he inculcated and the ideals he set up in the lives of the young men under his care. He was her own true son."

Immaculate Virgin, Mother of Jesus and our Mother, we believe in your triumphant assumption into heaven where the angels and saints acclaim you as Queen. We join them in praising you and bless the Lord who raised you above all creatures. With them we offer you our devotion and love. We are confident that you watch over our daily efforts and needs, and we take comfort from the faith in the coming resurrection. We look to you, our life, our sweetness, and our hope. After this earthly life, show us Jesus, the blest fruit of your womb, O kind, O loving, O sweet Virgin Mary.

Mother of Tenderness

The touching Byzantine image of Mary and the infant Jesus emphasizes the loving relationship between mother and child. Jesus has his little arms wrapped around his mother and his cheek pressed against Mary's. As for Mary, she clings to her child while looking out at the people—who are also her children.

This style of icon is known as Eleousa, or Mother of Tenderness. In the Eastern Church it is the most popular image of the Mother of God. By 1125 a Mother of Tenderness icon arrived in Russia. A large church was built to house the icon in the town of Vladimir, but in 1365, when a Mongol army threatened Moscow, the icon was carried to the Russian capital. Although the region around the city was devastated by the Mongol horde, Moscow was spared. This was a miracle in the eyes of the Russians, and they gave the Mother of Tenderness a new title, The Lady Who Saves Russia. After the miraculous deliverance of Moscow, both the Russian Orthodox Church and the czars looked upon the Mother of Tenderness as the special patron and protector of the church and the realm. The image is so lovely and evokes such a strong emotional response among Christians that reproductions of the Mother of Tenderness can be found all over the world. In this icon we see not only the deep bond of love that exists between Mary and Jesus, but also how dearly the Blessed Mother loves all of us and wishes to lead us to her son.

In dangers, in doubts, in difficulties, think of Mary, call upon Mary. Let not her name depart from your lips, never permit it to leave your heart. And that you may more certainly obtain the assistance of her prayers, do not neglect to walk in her footsteps.
—*From the Second Sermon of the Virgin Mother, St. Bernard of Clairvaux*

The oldest shrine of Our Lady in the Americas

In 1502 two brothers, Alfonso and Antonio Trejo, emigrated to the New World, settling in the island Columbus named Hispaniola in what is now the Dominican Republic. Among their possessions was a painting of the Blessed Virgin adoring the Christ Child in the manger while St. Joseph stands in the background. The brothers made their home in Higuey, and after several years offered their favorite painting to the parish church. The colonists venerated the image as Our Lady of Altagracia, or High Grace.

Over the years the painting has been richly embellished. Sometime in the eighteenth century it was placed in an intricate gold frame set with jewels. In 1922 Pope Pius XI honored Our Lady's image by sending it a gold crown. In 1979, Pope John Paul II hailed Altagracia as the first evangelizer of the Americas and personally set a gold and silver tiara on the painting.

Catholics of the Dominican Republic are deeply attached to Our Lady of Altagracia, venerating her as the patron of their country (they find it especially appealing that in the painting Mary wears blue, red, and white—the colors of the Dominican flag). But she is not theirs alone—this is the Madonna who blessed the faith when it was first planted in the New World and nurtured it as it spread across two continents.

Dearly beloved Mother, grant, if it be possible, that I may have no other spirit but thine to know Jesus and His divine will; that I may have no other soul but thine to praise and glorify the Lord; that I may have no other heart but thine to love God with a love as pure and ardent as thine. I do not ask thee for visions, revelations, sensible devotion, or spiritual pleasures. It is thy privilege to see God clearly; it is thy privilege to enjoy heavenly bliss; it is thy privilege to triumph gloriously in Heaven at the right hand of thy Son and to hold absolute sway over angels, men and demons; it is thy privilege to dispose of all the gifts of God, just as thou willest.

—*From a prayer of St. Louis de Montfort*

St. Elizabeth Ann Seton turns to Mary
for help, 1804

In 1804 Elizabeth Ann Seton, recently widowed and the mother of five young children, contemplated leaving the Episcopal church in which she had been raised and converting to the Catholic faith. A few months earlier, in Italy (where her husband had died), the notion had been so much clearer; surrounded on all sides by Catholic culture, living in a place where the Mass, the sacraments, and devotions to Our Lady and the saints were omnipresent, Elizabeth had felt becoming Catholic would be easy. But once she arrived home in New York City and realized how strongly her family, her friends, and New York society would oppose her decision, her constancy wavered. The more she read and debated within herself about what to do, the more confused she became.

One night she was saying evening prayers with her children when her eldest, nine-year-old Anna, asked Elizabeth to teach them a prayer she had heard her mother mention—the Hail Mary. All the other Seton children chimed in,

"Oh, do, Ma! Teach it to us!" And so Elizabeth Seton, still technically a Protestant, taught her children to pray to the Blessed Virgin.

"I asked my Savior," Elizabeth wrote at the time, "why should we not say it? If anyone is in Heaven, His Mother must be there." Then she added, "So I beg her with the tenderness and confidence of her child to pity us and guide us to the true faith."

O our sovereign Lady and our Advocate, commend us to thy Son. Grant, O blessed one, by the grace which thou hast merited, that He who through thee was graciously pleased to become a partaker in our infirmity and misery, may also, through thy intercession, make us partakers in His happiness and glory.

—*Prayer of St. Bernard of Clairvaux*

St. Thomas More visits the shrine of Our Lady of Willesden, 1534

By 1534 Henry VIII had cast out his wife, Catherine of Aragon, married his mistress, Anne Boleyn, broken away from the Roman Catholic Church, proclaimed himself Supreme Head of the Church in England, and issued a proclamation commanding all of his subjects to swear an oath recognizing his new marriage and his new authority over the church. St. Thomas More, the king's onetime friend and chancellor, had tried to keep his distance from these social and religious upheavals by never speaking on the subject. But for a man as internationally renowned as More, even his silence attracted attention. Realizing that his days as a free man were numbered, anxious about what might happen to his family, and afraid that he would not find the strength to remain true to his faith, More spent many sleepless nights praying and worrying.

In early April 1534 he made a pilgrimage to the shrine of Our Lady of Willesden outside central London to ask for Mary's help in the difficult times that were coming. Our Lady of Willesden was a local holy place, greatly beloved by Londoners like More. The focus of the shrine was a wooden sculpture of the Blessed Virgin that depicted her standing and presenting the infant Jesus to the world. A few weeks after making his petition to the Blessed Virgin, More was arrested.

In 1538, three years after St. Thomas was martyred, Henry VIII's commissioners burned the statue of Our Lady with many other sacred images. In 1885 a Catholic mission opened in Willesden, and in 1892 a replica of the original statue was installed in the parish church, where it is still venerated today.

O Immaculate Queen, Our Lady of Willesden, we consecrate ourselves and all we have and are to you forever in your holy Shrine. Make this Shrine glorious as of old. Bring pilgrims to worship at it. Convey their prayers to God in your own hands. Pray for us all. Pray for the conversion of all people to the religion of your Divine Son. And obtain pardon and mercy for our beloved Dead who have gone before us with the sign of faith and sleep the sleep of peace. Amen.

—*Prayer of Cardinal Francis Bourne*

DAY FOURTEEN
Our Lady of Fatima becomes Korea's Queen of Peace, 1953

At the end of World War II, when the Japanese occupation ended, Korea was divided in two: the north, under Russia's influence, became a Communist state, while the south, under the influence of the United States, opted for a democratic government. In 1950 North Korean forces attacked South Korea, sparking a civil war in which China, the United Nations, and the United States all took part.

By 1953 the casualties were staggering, with two million soldiers dead or wounded; there is no accurate number of Korean civilians killed or wounded, but the number was also in the millions. In this dark hour the Pilgrim Virgin of Fatima arrived in South Korea. The statue, a copy of the original enshrined in Fatima, Portugal, had been blessed by the bishop of Leira on October 13, 1947, the thirtieth anniversary of the Miracle of the Sun that marked the end of the visions of Lúcia dos Santos and her two cousins, Francisco and Jacinta Marto. The statue's custodians brought it to cities, towns, and countries around the globe, spreading the Fatima message of prayer and sacrifices for the conversion of sinners and for peace in the world.

During the statue's pilgrimage through South Korea the bishops of the country encouraged Korean Catholics to turn to Mary to bring an end to the war. Then, in a solemn ceremony, they crowned the statue of the Pilgrim Virgin, Korea's Queen of Peace.

In July 1953 North and South Korea signed a cease-fire.

Glorious Queen of peace, grant us peace in our hearts, harmony in our families and concord throughout the world. Immaculate Mother, as patron of our beloved country, watch over us and protect us with your motherly love. Amen.
—*From the prayer to the Immaculate Queen of Peace*

Raphael—Great Painter of the Madonna

No artist ever painted the Madonna more sweetly or more often than the Italian Renaissance master Raphael Sanzio. Although he died when he was only thirty-seven years old, Raphael painted the Virgin and Child at least twenty-one times, not to mention other Marian paintings such as *The Annunciation, Visitation, The Marriage of the Virgin,* and *Holy Family.* His *Sistine Madonna* and *Madonna of the Goldfinch* are among the most recognized and popular paintings of Mary and the Christ Child.

With Leonardo da Vinci and Michelangelo, Raphael is one of the giants of the Italian Renaissance. Even during his lifetime artists and art collectors knew he was a genius, which won him important commissions from Italy's wealthiest families, and even from the pope himself.

Raphael was born on April 6, 1483, and painted his first Madonna—actually, a scene of the Holy Family—when he was but seventeen years old. The next year he painted four Marian works:

The Coronation of the Virgin, The Annunciation, The Adoration of the Magi, and *The Presentation in the Temple.* By now he had found his style—bright, radiant colors; graceful, elegant poses for his figures; and the faces of Mary and the infant Jesus so lovely they stir the viewer's emotions. Almost overnight Raphael became one of the most popular artists in Italy—and it seemed that everyone wanted a Madonna.

During Holy Week in 1520 Raphael fell ill with a mysterious fever. He made his will, called for a priest to bring him last rites, and then died on his thirty-seventh birthday.

Mother of Mercy, pray for us.
Mary, Mother of God, pray for us.
Sweet Heart of Mary, be our hope
and our salvation.
Mary, my Mother, my hope, pray for us.

DAY SIXTEEN
St. Herman Joseph

It is said that as a boy Herman Joseph spent long hours in his parish church before a statue of the Virgin and Child, telling Mary and the Christ Child all of his childhood joys and woes as if the sculpted figures were living, breathing people. The stories go on to say that as a reward for his devotion, the statue came to life several times. Once when he offered an apple to Our Lady she reached out her hand to accept it. On another occasion when he came to show the Christ Child a new ball he had received as a gift, the infant Jesus climbed down from his mother's lap to play. And one winter, when times were especially hard for Herman Joseph's parents and he was going about barefoot, Our Lady told him where to find money for a pair of shoes.

Herman Joseph entered the Norbertine order as a teenager and was eventually ordained a priest. His innocence and goodness impressed some of his brother monks, and exasperated others. Few would consent to serve his Mass because Herman Joseph offered it with such reverence, often appearing to go into prolonged periods of ecstasy, that the service could last hours. And he never lost his deep affection for the Mother of God; he kept up the habit he had developed in childhood of spending long periods at her altar, although now he spent his time in prayer and contemplation rather than playing ball.

Hermann Joseph was over ninety years old when he died in 1241. Almost immediately the Norbertine monks and the people of Cologne venerated him as a saint. The formal canonization process for Herman Joseph was never completed, however, so in 1958 Pope Pius XII, in recognition of nearly seven hundred years of devotion to one of Mary's most faithful servants, granted Herman Joseph the title "Saint." His feast is celebrated on April 7.

The righteous flourish like the palm tree, and grow like a cedar in Lebanon. They are planted in the house of the LORD, they flourish in the courts of our God. They still bring forth fruit in old age.
—*Psalm 92:12–14*

In the neighborhood around Mount Etna in Sicily, people tell the story of a notorious bandit who terrorized the area nearly a thousand years ago, robbing and killing travelers, and even frightening townspeople to the point where they were afraid to step outside their doors at night.

On April 8, 1040, a violent earthquake shook the region around Mount Etna, causing avalanches on the mountainside, bringing down bell towers in the towns, and uprooting trees in the forest. The bandit, alone in the forest and afraid for his life, did something he hadn't done since he was a child—he called upon Our Lady for help. And Mary came. She appeared to him in the forest, stopped the earthquake, and then chided the reprobate for all the sins he had committed against God and man.

From that day the bandit became a changed man. He confessed all his sins to a priest and went back to the forest, where he built a small chapel and a hut where he spent the rest of his life as a hermit. He hung a Byzantine icon of the Blessed Virgin inside his chapel. This sacred image is enshrined today in the Church of St. Mary of the Valley near Messina.

> **Hail, O Steadfast Foundation of Faith!**
> **Hail, O Shining Emblem of Grace!**
> **Hail, O you through whom death was despoiled!**
> **Hail, O you through whom we were clothed with glory!**
> **Hail, O Bride and Maiden ever-pure!**
> *—From the Akathist Prayer to the Virgin*

DAY EIGHTEEN
The Wedding at Cana

The account in St. John's Gospel of the wedding feast at Cana (Jn. 2:1–11) is one of the most memorable miracle stories of the New Testament, in large part because the evangelist has given us so many intimate details of the event. You remember the story: Jesus and Mary and Jesus' disciples were invited to a wedding in the Galilean town of Cana. During what we would call the reception, the family ran out of wine—a situation as humiliating today as it was two thousand years ago. To spare the family—who must have been her friends—Mary goes to Jesus and says, "They have no wine." Notice that is all she says. She does not ask her son to perform a miracle—she tells him what is needed and then, perfectly confident that Christ will come to the aid of the bride and groom, Mary instructs the servants, "Do whatever he tells you."

What happens next is a sign not only of God's power but also of his generosity. Christ commands the servants to fill with water six stone jars, each of which could hold twenty or thirty gallons. "Now draw some out," he instructs one of the servants, "and take it to the steward of the feast." What the steward tastes is not water but wine—and fine wine at that. He is so impressed he compliments the groom, "You have kept the good wine until now." St. John concludes the story with the famous line, "This, the first of his signs, Jesus did at Cana in Galilee, and manifested his glory; and his disciples believed in him" (Jn. 2:11).

In this story we learn of the first instance on record of Our Lady's intercession. People are in need, she brings the situation to her son's attention, and he responds in a way the bride and groom never could have imagined. The miracle at Cana is the model of our relationship with Mary and her relationship with Christ.

Lord, now lettest thou thy servant depart in peace, according to thy word; for mine eyes have seen thy salvation which thou hast prepared in the presence of all peoples, a light for revelation to the Gentiles, and for glory to thy people Israel.
—Luke 2:29–32

St. Magdalen di Canossa

"After having experienced Mary's help on so many occasions," St. Magdalen di Canossa used to ask her sisters, "how can you be worried or afraid?"

Although she was born in 1774 as a marquesa and enjoyed great wealth, Magdalen's early life was wretched: her father died when she was five, and when her mother remarried she abandoned Magdalen and her four brothers to the care of tutors and governesses. Magdalen's own unhappy childhood made her especially sympathetic to orphaned and abandoned children. In her early twenties she began an ambitious program that ranged from providing meals to children who lived on the streets, to helping juvenile delinquents rebuild their lives, to teaching catechism classes to children who knew almost nothing about the Catholic faith. It was more than one woman could do, so she welcomed the help of like-minded women.

Under the patronage of Mary, whom she called the Mother of Charity beneath the Cross, St. Magdalen started the Canossian Sisters of

Charity to care for children. Magdalen and her nuns worked exclusively with girls, giving them an education, teaching them skills so they could find work, housing them in convent boarding schools so they would be safe, warm, well cared for, and loved. Their first foundation was in Verona, Magdalen's hometown; she opened a second house in Venice in 1812.

St. Magdalen was a practical, hardworking woman who had complete faith in God, took all her troubles to Our Lady, and found her consolation in Mass and Holy Communion. Today her sisters continue her work in twenty-one countries around the globe; her feast day is celebrated on April 10.

Virgin most prudent, pray for us.
Virgin most venerable, pray for us.
Virgin most renowned, pray for us.
Virgin most powerful, pray for us.
Virgin most merciful, pray for us.
Virgin most faithful, pray for us.
—*From the Litany of the Blessed Virgin*

Father Jacques Marquette, SJ, and the Mission of the Immaculate Conception, 1675

Stories of Father Jacques Marquette may lead you to think of him only as an explorer. Marquette and his fellow explorer Louis Joliet were the first Europeans to see, travel on, and chart the northern part of the Mississippi River. But whatever satisfaction Father Marquette derived from his travels, he had come to the New World as a missionary. He was still a Jesuit novice when he pleaded with his superior, "Order me to set out for foreign nations of which I have been thinking from my earliest boyhood." And in 1666, when he was twenty-nine years old, Father Marquette was sent to North America.

Like all of his brother Jesuits, Father Marquette had a strong devotion to the Blessed Virgin, particularly under her title the Immaculate Conception. In Marquette's day the church had not yet defined that doctrine, but the Jesuits were in the forefront of encouraging devotion to Mary's Immaculate Conception and using their considerable theological skills to convince the pope to issue a formal proclamation on the perpetual sinlessness of Mary. Jesuit missionaries routinely founded missions dedicated to the Immaculate Conception, and Father Marquette was no exception. In 1673 he stayed with the Illinois Native Americans in what is now the town of Kaskaskia. The tribe liked him and showed an interest in Christianity, but Marquette and Joliet were preparing for their journey on the Mississippi and the priest could not stay to found a mission. He promised he would come back.

True to his word, Marquette returned to Kaskaskia during Holy Week, 1675. On Holy Thursday he said Mass and preached before an impressive congregation: five hundred chiefs sat in a circle around him, while fifteen hundred warriors stood behind. Inspired by such a promising beginning Father Marquette founded a mission among the Illinois, dedicating it to the Immaculate Conception.

I will greatly rejoice in the LORD, my soul shall exult in my God; for he has clothed me with the garments of salvation, he has covered me with the robe of righteousness,

as a bridegroom decks himself with a garland, as a bride adorns herself with her jewels. So the Lord GOD will cause righteousness and praise to spring forth before all the nations.

—*Isaiah 61:10–11*

DAY TWENTY-ONE
The New York World's Fair and Michelangelo's Pietà, 1964

One of the thrills for visitors to the 1964–1965 World's Fair in Flushing Meadow, Queens, was the chance to visit the pavilion displays set up by dozens of different countries to showcase the most exciting, eye-catching treasures from their homeland. On April 12, 1964, the Vatican opened its own pavilion at the fair, and the treasure the Holy Father sent to New York was none other than Michelangelo's *Pietà*.

The fair's organizers, and the millions who planned to visit it, were thrilled, but in Italy the decision set off an outpouring of protests. The sculpture was a priceless national treasure; it had never left Italy before. What if it were damaged in transit? Or worse, since it was traveling to the United States by ship, what if it were lost at sea? Finally, did this classic representation of the dead Christ in the arms of his sorrowful mother belong at such a glitzy commercial venture?

In the end, all such anxieties were assuaged. The ship did not sink; the sculpture was not damaged; and designers of the Vatican pavilion created a darkened room where spotlights lit up Michelangelo's masterpiece as Gregorian chant played softly in the background. It was a setting that moved even the most secular tourist to reverence.

During his whirlwind visit to New York City in October 1965, Pope Paul VI viewed the *Pietà* at the World's Fair. Afterward, he made the people of Italy a promise: the *Pietà* would never leave home again.

Holy Mary, the Queen of Heaven, and Mistress of the world, stood by the cross of Our Lord Jesus Christ, full of sadness.

All you who pass by the way, look and see if there is any sorrow like my sorrow.
—*Lamentations 1:12*

DAY TWENTY-TWO
Venetians acquire the icon of the Virgin
Nicopeia in Constantinople, 1204

One of the saddest days in the history of Christendom occurred on April 13, 1204, when crusaders from Western Europe attacked Constantinople, committing acts of murder, sacrilege, and destruction that devastated what had been the greatest Christian city in the East. The Venetians among the crusaders kept aloof from the rioting, but they did plunder the city. Realizing that Constantinople's churches and palaces were filled with rare treasures, the Venetians collected the best, the most beautiful, and the holiest objects they could find before they were damaged or destroyed by marauding mobs.

The Venetians wanted one icon in particular— the Virgin Nicopeia, or Bringer of Victory. Desirous of having Mary's protection over their city, the Venetians stole the icon, carried it home, and placed it in a chapel in the Basilica of St. Mark. It is still there, and is the focus of Marian devotion. Each Sunday afternoon after vespers at St. Mark's, the congregation processes through the church to the chapel of the Nicopeia, chanting the Litany of the Blessed Virgin. In a church that is also a prime tourist attraction, the clergy of St. Mark's have roped off the Nicopeia chapel as holy ground reserved for visitors who have come to pray.

Over the centuries, devotion to Our Lady of Victory has evolved; it is no longer limited to seeking victory on a battlefield. Today Christians are much more likely to ask Our Lady to grant them victory over temptation, sickness, poverty, and all the day-to-day anxieties of life. Certainly that is how the Nicopeia icon is venerated in Venice, where Mary's chapel is crowded at all hours of the day with people who bring their troubles to the Mother of God and ask for her help in overcoming them.

Triumphant in Thy Joys, pray for us.
Triumphant in Thy Entrance into the Heavenly Jerusalem, pray for us.
Triumphant in the Angels Who Remained Faithful, pray for us.
Triumphant in the Felicity of the Blessed, pray for us.
—*From the Litany of Our Lady of Victory*

Bishop Francis X. Ford and Sister Joan Marie of Maryknoll are imprisoned in China, 1950

For most of its history the United States was considered mission territory for the church, but by the early twentieth century the Catholic Church in America was generating so many vocations that it could send its own priests, brothers, and nuns to overseas mission fields. In 1911 two priests, Father James A. Walsh of New York and Father Thomas F. Price of North Carolina, teamed up to form a missionary order dedicated to Our Lady for the foreign missions, particularly China. They acquired property on a hilltop outside the Hudson River town of Ossining, New York, and named the place Maryknoll, which also became the name of their mission society.

In 1918 the first graduating class of three priests, Father James Walsh (nephew of the founder), Father Bernard Meyer, and Father Francis X. Ford, were sent to China. Father Ford opened the first Maryknoll seminary in China in 1921, and in 1935 he was consecrated a bishop. When the Communists seized power in China they ordered all foreign missionaries out of the country; like many Maryknoll missionaries, Bishop Ford refused to go. In 1950 Bishop Ford and his secretary, Maryknoll Sister Joan Marie, were arrested. Each was kept in solitary confinement for nearly four months, and then they were led like criminals through the streets to a prison in Canton.

After a show trial, Bishop Ford was tortured to death in prison. Some days or weeks later, Sister Joan Marie was taken to see his grave and then expelled from China.

Remember, O most gracious Virgin Mary, that never was it known that anyone who fled to thy protection, implored thy help, or sought thy intercession, was left unaided. Inspired with this confidence I fly unto thee, O Virgin of virgins, my Mother. To thee I come; before thee I stand, sinful and sorrowful. O Mother of the Word Incarnate, despise not my petitions, but in thy mercy hear and answer me. Amen.
—*The Memorare*

Our Lady of Kiev

Vladimir, prince of Kiev in what is now the Ukraine, killed his brother, kept seven wives and hundreds of concubines, and once consecrated a pagan temple with human sacrifice. When this ruthless, bloody-minded man agreed to be baptized to cement an alliance with the emperor in Constantinople, no one in Byzantium or Kiev expected Vladimir to take the ceremony seriously. Yet, after his baptism, Vladimir truly was a new man. He dismissed his wives and his harem, tore down his pagan temple, and destroyed the idols. He took as his one and only wife the emperor's sister, Anna. And when he returned home he brought with him a small crowd of bishops and priests, and wagons filled with icons, sacred vessels, Bibles, and liturgical books—everything necessary to begin the conversion of his people. Back in Kiev, Vladimir set the example of Christian living, feeding the poor and the helpless every day at his own residence, caring for the sick, and even outlawing the death penalty. He dedicated the first church he built in Kiev to

Mary's Assumption, but it became known as the Tithe Church because Vladimir pledged 10 percent of his annual income to the decoration and maintenance of this church.

Among the icons Vladimir brought from Constantinople was one of the Blessed Virgin. At a place along the Dneiper River called Kieff, where hundreds of his people had been baptized, Vladimir erected a church and then presented this icon to the priests.

> Hail, O you who unthroned the Enemy of Men!
> Hail, O you who showed forth Christ the Lord, Lover of Mankind!
> Hail, O you who cleansed us from the stain of pagan worship!
> Hail, O you who saved us from the mire of evil deeds!
> Hail, O you who guide the faithful toward wisdom!
> Hail, O you, Delight of all the Nations!
> Hail, O Bride and Maiden ever-pure!
> —*From the Akathist hymn to the Blessed Virgin*

DAY TWENTY-FIVE
Remembering St. Bernadette Soubirous

St. Bernadette's visions of Our Lady at the grotto outside Lourdes made her the focus of unwanted attention. Pilgrims sought her out to bless them or their rosaries, or to give her money or other gifts. To her credit, Bernadette refused everything offered her and would not bless anyone or anything. To escape, Bernadette entered a convent boarding school. In 1866 she asked to join the Sisters of Notre Dame of Nevers; as just one nun among many she hoped to become almost as anonymous as she had been before Mary appeared to her. She once likened herself to a common broom. "Our Lady used me," she said. "They have put me back in my corner. I am happy to stay there."

In 1876 Bernadette considered attending the dedication of the new shrine basilica at Lourdes, but the thought of being mobbed by pilgrims frightened and dissuaded her. And so she stayed in the convent, only venturing out to nurse soldiers during the Franco-Prussian War of 1870–1871. Many saints have said they found humility a difficult virtue to acquire, yet St. Bernadette had it in abundance.

Her health, which had never been good, continued to decline while she was in the convent. She suffered from asthma, and eventually she developed tuberculosis of the bones, a terribly painful disease that she endured with courage. When Bernadette was declared a saint it was for her humility, her striving to be truly holy, her fidelity to the rule of her religious community. Her visions made Bernadette a celebrity, but her virtues made her a saint. Her feast day is celebrated each year on April 16.

By appearing in the Grotto of Lourdes, you were pleased to make it a privileged sanctuary, whence you dispense your favors; and already many sufferers have obtained the cure of their infirmities, both spiritual and corporal. I come, therefore, with complete confidence to implore your maternal intercession. Obtain, O loving Mother, the grant of my requests. Through gratitude for your favors, I will endeavor to imitate your virtues, that I may one day share your glory. Amen.

—*From the Prayer to Our Lady of Lourdes*

The Salve Regina

I f you've ever made a retreat in a convent or a monastery, you've likely heard the nuns and monks sing "Salve Regina, Hail Holy Queen," as the final prayer of the day. In some places it is customary to sing this hymn as the community files out of the chapel. It is a lovely melody, one of the loveliest in the entire repertory of Gregorian chant, and hearing it sung never fails to touch the mind and heart. There is something inexpressibly beautiful about praising Mary at the end of a long day, of placing ourselves under the protection of she who is "our life, our sweetness, and our hope."

The prayer is an old one—nine hundred years old, to be precise. It was written by a German monk, Blessed Herman the Lame (1013–1054). Herman was born with malformed legs; he learned to walk eventually, but only in a halting, limping manner. In spite of his disability, he possessed a host of other gifts. He had a brilliant mind that could sort out the thorniest theological problem. He was a gifted musician who could sing, play instruments, and even compose music. After he entered the Abbey of Reichenau, Herman wrote new hymns for his brother monks, including "Salve Regina." From childhood he had had a special love for Our Lady, and he expressed that love in a sublime hymn.

In "Salve Regina, Hail Holy Queen," Blessed Herman articulated beautifully what all the faithful know—that Mary is a loving mother who extends her mercy and compassion to us all.

Hail holy Queen! Mother of mercy, our life, our sweetness, and our hope! To thee do we cry, poor banished children of Eve; to thee do we send up our sighs, mourning and weeping in this valley of tears. Turn then, O most gracious advocate, thine eyes of mercy toward us. And after this, our exile, show unto us the blessed fruit of thy womb, Jesus. O clement, O loving, O most sweet Virgin Mary.

DAY TWENTY-SEVEN
Old St. Mary's, Chicago

In his very first pastoral letter, published in 1792, the first Catholic bishop of the United States, John Carroll, said to his clergy, "I shall only add this my earnest request, that to the exercise of the sublimest virtues, faith, hope, and charity, you will join a fervent and well regulated devotion to the Holy Mother of our Lord and Savior Jesus Christ; that you will place great confidence in Her intercession; and have recourse to Her in all your necessities." Bishop Carroll was only re-emphasizing a devotion to and trust in Our Lady that was as old as the discovery of America itself— after all, Christopher Columbus had named his flagship the *Santa Maria.*

In the early years of the nineteenth century the necessities of the Catholics of Chicago were enormous—they had no recourse at all to the Mass or the sacraments. The man who founded Chicago in 1779, Jean Baptiste Point du Sable, was a Catholic, but his settlement was too tiny to become a full-fledged parish at a time when priests in the United States were scarce. It was not until 1833 that Joseph Rosati, bishop of

St. Louis (his diocese included Illinois), responded to a petition from 128 Catholics in the town and sent the newly ordained Father John St. Cyr to establish Chicago's first parish.

On May 1, Father St. Cyr said Mass in a log building—the first home of Chicago's first parish. The building was dedicated to St. Mary of the Assumption—a sign not only of Marian devotion in the Chicago "wilderness," but also of that confidence in Mary's help that Bishop Carroll had urged upon his priests and people forty-one years earlier. As the mother church of the archdiocese, the parish came to be known affectionately as Old St. Mary's. In the succeeding years Chicago's trust in Mary has been richly rewarded—the Archdiocese of Chicago is one of the largest in the nation, serving over 2.3 million of the faithful in more than 350 parishes.

As a little child, I loved you like a mother. Now that I am old, my love for you has grown. Receive me in heaven as one of the blessed, and I will proclaim that I have obtained such a great prize through your patronage. Amen.
—*Prayer of Pope Leo XIII*

Our Lady liberates Uruguay, 1825

In Uruguay, Mary is the patron of the country's independence movement. On April 19, 1825, thirty-three Uruguayan patriots who had been exiled from their country landed at Agraciada. They went immediately to the town of Florida, to the parish church where a small wooden sculpture of the Blessed Virgin was venerated. There they knelt and asked Mary to intercede for them and for the future happiness of their country.

On August 25 Uruguay proclaimed its independence from Brazil (which had annexed Uruguay four years earlier). The delegates to the Constitutional Court signed the Act of Independence, and then they all went to the little church in Florida to thank Mary for her help and to beg for her blessing on the people of Uruguay.

In 1857 the national government proclaimed Mary Liberator of Uruguay and placed a crown of gold and jewels upon the statue. The image itself, about sixteen inches high, is lovely and represents Mary's Assumption. It was carved in the eighteenth century by a Guarani Indian at one of the Jesuit missions in Paraguay. Today the traditional prayer to Our Lady of the Thirty-Three reminds Mary, "Before your image our founders bent their knees and inclined their flag." It implores Mary to "protect our country which was born beneath your shadow."

In 1961 Blessed Pope John XXIII recognized Our Lady of the Thirty-Three as the national patron of Uruguay. In 1975, during the country's 150th anniversary celebrations, both the statue and the church where it is venerated were declared national historic monuments.

The princess is decked in her chamber with gold-woven robes; in many-colored robes she is led to the king, with her virgin companions, her escort, in her train. With joy and gladness they are led along as they enter the palace of the king. I will cause your name to be celebrated in all generations; therefore the peoples will praise you for ever and ever.

—*Psalm 45:13–15, 17*

Marian societies around the world

In 1962 there were ninety thousand Marian sodalities, or societies, around the world, with eighteen thousand of those within the United States. These organizations for laypeople included men's, women's, and children's groups and organizations, as well as sodalities for high school and college students. Their goals were all the same—to foster love for Mary, to grow in personal holiness, and to participate in activities that would assist the church and help one's neighbor through works of charity.

Religious orders such as the Jesuits, the Dominicans, and the Carmelites organized sodalities outside of parishes, but they existed within parish organizations, too. The Society of St. Vincent de Paul, whose members quietly go about their work assisting the needy in their own parish, falls into the category of a sodality; so do purgatorial societies whose members pray daily for souls of the departed. But sodalities affiliated with Our Lady have always been the most popular. Pope Benedict XIV, one of many popes who encouraged Catholics to join a sodality of Mary, once said that as members of a sodality Christians "are taught to strive after the height of Christian perfection and to press forward to the goal of eternal salvation."

The greatest number of these Marian groups encourage their members to commit themselves to a particular religious practice that will draw them closer to Mary, such as daily recitation of the rosary or wearing the scapular of Our Lady of Mount Carmel.

Sodalities of Our Lady have enjoyed a very impressive membership: Charles Borromeo, Francis de Sales, Alphonsus Liguori, Madeliene Sophie Barat, Bernadette Suobirous, and Therese the Little Flower all joined Marian sodalities before they became saints.

> **O Mary, conceived without sin, pray for us who have recourse to thee.**
> **Holy Mary, pray for us!**
> **Immaculate Heart of Mary, pray for us now and at the hour of our death.**
> **Sweet Heart of Mary, be my salvation!**
> **Our Lady, Queen of Peace, pray for us!**
> —*Favorite brief prayers of St. Alphonsus Liguori*

Father Eusebio Kino in the American Southwest

Born in northern Italy, Eusebio Kino joined the Jesuits hoping he would be sent to the missions in Asia; instead his superiors assigned him to the region known today as northern Mexico and southern Arizona. In the Sonora region of northern Mexico he was often at odds with Spanish mine owners over the wretched living and working conditions of the Native Americans who labored in the silver mines.

Like so many missionaries, Father Kino had a profound love for and confidence in Mary. He named the first mission he founded among the Native Americans of Arizona for Mary—Our Lady of Sorrows. He established the mission in 1687 among the Pima tribe, and his first convert was a chief named Coxi. Our Lady's mission became his headquarters; over the next twenty-three years Father Kino set out on forty expeditions covering fifty thousand square miles throughout the American Southwest. He founded twenty more missions, including the famous San Xavier del Bac, which is still a working parish, outside Tucson, Arizona. He also established ranches where he taught the Native Americans how to improve their lives by adopting advanced methods of farming and raising livestock. His genuine love for the native people of the Southwest, his gift for languages, and his genius in presenting Christianity in a way that the Native Americans found appealing and accessible, all combined to make Father Kino a very successful missionary. By the time of his death he had converted four thousand Native Americans.

LORD**, thou hast been our dwelling place in all generations. Before the mountains were brought forth, or ever thou hadst formed the earth and the world, from everlasting to everlasting thou art God.**
—*Psalm 90:1–2*

DAY THIRTY-ONE
St. Louis de Montfort's Total Consecration to Mary

The spirituality of St. Louis de Montfort (1673–1716) was based on living his entire life "with Mary, in Mary, through Mary, and for Mary." He took as his model the child Jesus, who like every other child relied on his mother for everything—love, food, clothing, comfort, knowledge. Montfort urged his readers to become like the young Jesus and have confidence that Mary, our spiritual mother, will provide us with everything we need.

Montfort regarded the act of consecration as a kind of renewal of our baptismal vows, when we offered ourselves completely to God and became his children. In this new consecration we offer ourselves again to God, this time through Mary. But the consecration to Mary isn't something abstract, we are meant to live it out in day-to-day life by trying to imitate her virtues of humility, patience, love, and complete faith in God. "It all comes to this, then, " St. Louis wrote. "We must discover a simple means to obtain from God the grace needed to become holy. It is precisely this

I wish to teach you. My contention is that you must first discover Mary if you would obtain this grace from God." Finally, de Montfort reminds us that among all the saints we can have no better helper than Mary: we can feel at ease approaching her because she is human, and we can be confident that God will listen to her prayers because, unlike us, she is sinless.

Hail Mary, beloved Daughter of the Eternal Father. Hail Mary, admirable Mother of the Son. Hail Mary, faithful Spouse of the Holy Ghost. Hail Mary, my Mother, my loving Mistress, my powerful sovereign. Hail, my joy, my glory, my heart and my soul. Thou art all mine by mercy, and I am thine by justice. But I am not yet sufficiently thine. I now give myself wholly to thee without keeping anything back for myself or others. If thou seest anything in me which does not belong to thee, I beseech thee to take it and make thyself the absolute Mistress of all that is mine.

—*From St. Louis de Montfort's Prayer to Mary*

St. Mary's, the first seminary in the United States

When Pope Pius VI named Father John Carroll the first bishop of the United States, with the entire country as his diocese, there were about 28,000 Catholics in the country, served by 24 priests. There were no Catholic schools, no nuns, no seminaries—in other words, almost nothing existed to promote the growth of the church in the United States. About the same time, the French Revolution had driven the Sulpician Fathers from their seminaries in France. The Catholic Church in the United States needed a seminary; the Sulpicians needed a home, so Bishop Carroll invited several French priests to Baltimore to train American men for the priesthood.

Carroll purchased a disused inn outside Baltimore, called the One Mile Tavern, to house his seminary. He dedicated it to Mary, the help of Christians. He once wrote to a friend, "I have been attached to the practice of devotion to the Blessed Virgin Mary…. I have established it among my people, and I have placed my diocese under her protection." In October 1791 classes began with four students.

The church in the United States had so many needs that Bishop Carroll and the faculty of St. Mary's learned to be flexible. They opened satellite schools for French-, Spanish-, and German-speaking Catholics. St. Elizabeth Ann Seton opened a Catholic elementary school in a room in the seminary's chapel, also named St. Mary's. A few years later St. Mary's opened its doors to Mother Elizabeth Lange's school for black Catholic children. For decades St. Mary's has trained so many men for the priesthood that there is scarcely a diocese in the country not served by an alumnus of Our Lady's seminary in Baltimore.

O Mother of men and peoples, you know all their sufferings and their hopes, you feel in a motherly way all the struggles between good and evil, between the light and the darkness which shakes the world— accept our cry addressed in the Holy Spirit directly to your heart and embrace with the love of the Mother and the Handmaid of the Lord the peoples who await this embrace the most, and likewise the peoples whose consecration you too are particularly awaiting. Take under your motherly protection the whole human family which we can consecrate to you, O mother, with affectionate rapture. May the time of peace and freedom, the time of truth, justice and hope, approach for everyone.

—*From a prayer of Pope John Paul II*

In 1370 a storm blew up off the coast of Sardinia. Sailors aboard a merchant vessel tried to save their ship by unloading the cargo. They had just pushed a large crate into the sea when the storm came to an abrupt end. The sailors were curious about what might have been in the crate, but before they could retrieve it the current carried the crate away.

It came ashore in Sardinia, where it was salvaged by some Mercy Fathers. Upon prying open the lid, the priests found a painted wooden sculpture of the Virgin and Child inside. They carried the sculpture back to their church, where someone, either a member of the religious community or one the townspeople, recalled that when the church had been built forty years earlier, one of the priests assigned to the parish had predicted that someday "a great lady" would come to dwell there, and at her coming malaria would vanish from the neighborhood. Everyone standing around the statue wondered if this sculpture of Mary was the great lady of the prediction.

The Mercy Fathers found a prominent place for the statue in their church, and the townspeople came often to pray before it. As it happened, the region was plagued by malaria. After the arrival of the statue, however, no new cases of malaria were reported. Since *malaria* means "bad air" in Italian, the statue became known as Our Lady of Bonaria, or Good Air—only one example of the good things that Mary secures for people who place their confidence in her intercession. In 1908, in recognition of centuries of devotion, Pope St. Pius X proclaimed Our Lady of Bonaria patron of Sardinia.

It is sweet music to the ear to say: I honor you, O Mother! It is a sweet song to repeat: I honor you, O holy Mother! You are my delight, dear hope, and chaste love, my strength in all adversities. If my spirit is troubled and stricken by passions, if it suffers from the painful burden of sadness and weeping, if you see your child overwhelmed by misfortune, O gracious Virgin Mary, you let me find rest in your motherly embrace.
—*Prayer of Pope Leo XIII*

DAY THIRTY-FOUR
The Rosary

Everyone has seen a rosary—the most recognized object of Catholic devotional life. Saints, popes, and ordinary laymen and laywomen have promoted the rosary for centuries. In recent times psychologists have even "prescribed" it as a way to reduce the stress and anxiety of daily life.

Tradition says that Our Lady gave the rosary to St. Dominic in the thirteenth century. Certainly the Dominicans have long been at the forefront of encouraging Catholics to pray the rosary often— every day, if possible. But the string of prayer beads predates St. Dominic by many years. Hermits in the deserts of Egypt kept track of how many Our Fathers they had prayed by using a string of beads. Greek monks used a string of beads to keep count of how many times they made the sign of the cross or prostrated themselves.

It was the Dominicans, however, who gave us the rosary in its present form—ten small beads on which to pray the Hail Mary separated by a larger bead on which to pray the Our Father. The Dominicans also encouraged the faithful to meditate on a mystery or event from the life of Our Lord or Our Lady as they prayed each decade (a section of ten beads). This was a dramatic development because it elevated the rosary from a simple counting tool to a devotional object that combined active prayer with meditation.

There are four sets of mysteries: the Joyful, which focuses on Christ's coming into the world; the Luminous, introduced by Pope John Paul II to contemplate Christ's ministry; the Sorrowful, which meditates on Jesus' sufferings and death; and the Glorious, which celebrate the glories of Jesus and Mary. As Pope Leo XIII wrote in 1894, "No man can meditate upon these without feeling a new awakening in his heart of confidence that he will certainly obtain through Mary the fullness of the mercies of God."

O God, whose only begotten Son, by his life, death, and resurrection, has purchased for us the reward of eternal salvation, grant, we beseech thee, that meditating on these mysteries in the most holy rosary of the Blessed Virgin Mary, we may both imitate what they contain and obtain what they promise.

Our Lady of Good Counsel

It was St. Augustine who first acclaimed Mary as "the counsel of the Apostles," the Mother who continues to guide the church and all people to her son. This idea of Mary has been expressed in a tangible way in a painting of the Virgin and Child that has come to be known as *Our Lady of Good Counsel*.

The painting was discovered in 1467 in the town of Genazzano, about thirty miles south of Rome, by workmen who were renovating the parish church. It is a small image, fifteen inches tall and seventeen inches wide, painted on an eggshell-thin fragment of plaster. That it didn't crumble when the workmen picked it up could be the first miracle of Mary of Good Counsel.

Townspeople came to the church to see the image, first out of curiosity, then out of devotion. Soon there were reports of extraordinary graces granted through Mary's intercession. The town notary recorded that within sixteen weeks of the discovery of the sacred image, people in Genazzano and the surrounding countryside reported 171 miracles wrought by Our Lady of Good Counsel.

Undoubtedly because of her name, Good Counsel, many popes have turned to Mary under this title, praying her to grant them the wisdom to govern the church as Christ would wish. In 1680 Urban VIII made the first papal pilgrimage to the shrine. Blessed Pius IX went in 1864, and Blessed John XXIII in 1959. When he was elected pope in 1939, as the world stood on the brink of war, Pius XII placed his entire pontificate under the protection of Our Lady of Good Counsel, echoing what his predecessor, Pope Leo XIII, had said, "Children, follow her counsels."

To you, O Mary, are known all the needs of your people and of the whole Church. Mother of Truth and Seat of Wisdom, dissipate the clouds of error which darken our minds. Amend the strayings of our hearts and inspire in us love for truth and the desire to do good. Obtain for all people a holy fear of God so that society may know happiness. Give us lively faith that we may trust in those things which are imperishable. Give us that love

which is sealed forever in God. Obtain for families fidelity, harmony, and peace. Stir up and confirm in the hearts of those who govern nations a clear notion of their responsibility, and of their duty to foster religion, morality, and the common good.

—*From a prayer of Pope Pius XII*

DAY THIRTY-SIX
Pope Benedict XV adds "Queen of Peace" to the Litany of the Blessed Virgin, 1917

The Litany of the Blessed Virgin is also known as the Litany of Loreto because it originated at that Marian shrine sometime before 1558. There were earlier litanies of Mary, most famously the Akathist of the Blessed Virgin, which is popular in the Eastern Church and was probably written down in the seventh century.

The litany invokes Our Lady under her various titles and mystical attributes—Seat of Wisdom, Cause of Our Joy, Gate of Heaven, Refuge of Sinners. Praying the litany is like reciting spiritual poetry.

Over the years, to mark momentous events or to encourage renewed devotion to Mary, popes have added new invocations to the litany. Blessed Pius IX, who defined the doctrine of the Immaculate Conception, added the invocation, "Queen conceived without original sin." Leo XIII, a great proponent of the rosary, added "Queen of the most holy Rosary." Pius XII, who defined the doctrine of Mary's Assumption, added, "Queen assumed into heaven." Pope John Paul II, fulfilling the desire of the fathers of the Second Vatican Council added, "Mother of the church."

As the devastation of World War I spread across the globe, a heart-sick Pope Benedict XV wrote to a friend that he would add to Mary's Litany the prayer, "Queen of peace, pray for us."

Queen of virgins, pray for us.
Queen of all saints, pray for us.
Queen conceived without original sin,
pray for us.
Queen assumed into heaven, pray for us.
Queen of the most holy Rosary,
pray for us.
Queen of families, pray for us.
Queen of peace, pray for us.
—*From the Litany of the Blessed Virgin*

Miracles of Our Lady of Quito

The city of Quito, located high in the Andes Mountains, has always suffered from earthquakes, some of them very severe. For four hundred years the people of Quito have prayed to Mary to protect them from such natural disasters.

The painting of Our Lady of Quito is displayed in the city's cathedral. In 1874 a remarkable event took place before Mary's shrine. Gabriel García Moreno, the president of Ecuador, was joined by a throng of ecclesiastical and government officials as he knelt before Our Lady of Quito and read aloud this prayer, "Prostrate before your divine presence, all the public powers of the Church and of the State offer and consecrate to Thee now and for always the republic of Ecuador as Thy exclusive possession and property."

About thirty years later a copy of this painting hung in the dining hall of the Jesuit College in Quito. On April 20, 1906, thiry-five students ranging in age from eleven to seventeen, a Jesuit priest, a Jesuit brother, three school employees, and two visitors were having coffee and chatting in the dining hall when some of the boys claimed that the picture had come to life and Mary's eyes were moving. Everyone came forward to look at the picture, and all were surprised to see that the eyes were opening and closing. The phenomenon ended after about fifteen minutes, but the picture has been a focus of devotion in Ecuador ever since. Recently, it was taken to every major city in the country before returning to Quito to be enshrined in the Compañia, the Jesuit church.

O Virgin Mary, our Mother preeminent
above all on earth.
Come to our assistance and show us mercy,
because thou art our Mother.

Above all others, thou wert attentive to the
Word of the Father, Who doth great things
in thy honor.
Come to our assistance and show us mercy,
because thou art our Mother.

Thou art the most worthy temple of the
Most Holy Trinity.

Come to our assistance and show us mercy,
because thou art our Mother.

In thee is that same purity the Angels enjoy.
Come to our assistance and show us mercy,
because thou art our Mother.

The Christian world proclaims that thou
dost reign on the right side of the
King of Kings.
Come to our assistance and show us mercy,
because thou art our Mother.
—*From the Novena to Our Lady of Quito*

Pope Paul VI publishes a letter on devotions to Mary during the month of May, 1965

The Second Vatican Council was still in session when Pope Paul VI published *Mense Maio,* his letter praising the age-old tradition of dedicating the month of May as a special month of prayer and processions in honor of the Virgin Mary.

"Our heart rejoices at the thought of the moving tribute of faith and love which will soon be paid to the Queen of Heaven in every corner of the earth," Paul VI wrote. "For this is the month during which Christians, in their churches and their homes, offer the Virgin Mother more fervent and loving acts of homage and veneration; and it is the month in which a greater abundance of God's merciful gifts comes down to us from our Mother's throne."

The pope asked the faithful to pray to Mary during May for the success of the Council, but most especially for peace throughout the world. In 1965 the world was in the depths of the Cold War and the nuclear arms race; the first U.S. forces had arrived in Vietnam; and tensions between Israel and the Arab nations were running high.

"In this pitiful state of affairs," the pope said, "let us offer our pleas to the Mother of God with greater devotion and confidence, so that we may obtain her favor and her blessings."

The May Magnificat

MAY is Mary's month, and I
Muse at that and wonder why:
    Her feasts follow reason,
    Dated due to season—

Candlemas, Lady Day;
But the Lady Month, May,
    Why fasten that upon her,
    With a feasting in her honour?

Is it only its being brighter
Than the most are must delight her?
    Is it opportunest
    And flowers finds soonest?

. . .

This ecstasy all through mothering earth
Tells Mary her mirth till Christ's birth
    To remember and exultation
    In God who was her salvation.
—*From the poem by Gerard Manley Hopkins*

Our Lady of Africa

A statue of Mary, dark-skinned like the people of North Africa, was first brought to Algeria in 1873 by Charles-Martial-Allemand Lavigerie, bishop of Algiers and founder of the missionary order known as the White Fathers and the White Sisters. The statue was installed in the Basilica of Our Lady of Africa in Algiers, a magnificent church built in the Moorish style. In keeping with European tradition, the statue is dressed in a white gown and blue velvet robe heavily embroidered with gold. On its head, the statue wears a gold crown made by Muslim artisans in the town of Tlemcen.

During his twenty-five years in Algeria, Bishop Lavigerie worked for two things: the conversion of the Muslim population and the abolition of the slave trade that was still flourishing in Africa in the late nineteenth century. He entrusted both objectives to Our Lady of Africa. Whenever he addressed the White Fathers, Lavigerie always said, "Have recourse to Our Lord and to Our Lady of Africa."

In spite of violent upheaval in recent years and the difficulty of life for Algerian Christians, the basilica and the statue of Our Lady of Africa both remain in Algiers today.

I am very dark, but comely,
O daughters of Jerusalem.
I am a rose of Sharon, a lily of the valleys.
As a lily among brambles,
so is my love among maidens.
—*Song of Solomon 1:5; 2:1–2*

DAY FORTY
The Ascension

Forty days after his resurrection, as he stood in the presence of his apostles and his Blessed Mother, Christ ascended back into heaven. It was only right that Mary should have been there—as Mother and Son they were inextricably linked together. Aside from the story of the finding in the temple (Lk. 2:41–52), Christ's childhood and the "hidden years" before he began his public ministry are entirely unknown to us, and were probably unknown to the apostles. But Mary knew every detail and, as St. Luke's Gospel tells us, "pondered them in her heart."

We could go so far as to say she had to be a witness to the Ascension because it brought the story of salvation full circle: thirty-three years earlier the Holy Spirit had descended upon her at the Annunciation and "the Word was made flesh;" now she sees the Word return to heaven, but only after he has left Mary and the apostles and all believers with this promise, "Lo, I am with you always" (Mt. 28:20).

With Christ no longer personally present among them, it must have been a great consolation for the apostles to still be able to gather around Mary. They set the example for us, for the faithful in every age, of drawing close to Mary, who will always teach us how to draw even closer to Jesus Christ. In the document *Lumen Gentium*, the Fathers of the Second Vatican Council wrote, "The Mother of Jesus, in the glory which she possesses in body and soul in heaven, is the image and beginning of the Church as it is to be perfected in the world to come. Likewise she shines forth on earth until the day of the Lord shall come, a sign of certain hope and comfort to the pilgrim People of God."

I give thee thanks, O LORD, with my whole heart; in the sight of the angels I sing thy praise; I bow down toward thy holy temple and give thanks to thy name for thy steadfast love and thy faithfulness; for thou hast exalted above everything thy name and thy word. On the day I called thou didst answer me, my strength of soul thou didst increase.

—Psalm 138:1–3

St. Catherine Labouré and the Miraculous Medal

At her baptism she was named Zoe, and she was eighth of ten children born to French farmers Pierre and Madeleine Labouré. For some reason her parents did not send Zoe to school (although all her brothers and sisters went). Later in life she did learn to read and write, but she was never at ease when she had to read aloud or write a letter.

When Zoe was eight her mother died, and soon thereafter an older sister entered a convent. Pierre Labouré expected Zoe to act as housekeeper and help him raise the children. In her teens, when Zoe announced that she wanted to become a nun too, her father refused to give his consent. Hoping to get the idea of the convent out of her head, he sent her to Paris to work as a waitress in her uncle's café. But Zoe's desire for the religious life did not go away, and eventually Pierre gave in to her wishes.

She joined the Sisters of Charity of St. Vincent de Paul, taking the name Catherine. In 1830, four days after she arrived as a novice at the order's convent on Paris's Rue du Bac Catherine had her first vision of the Virgin Mary. Out of these visions emerged a new Catholic sacramental, the Miraculous Medal. In a letter to her confessor in which she described her visions of Our Lady, St. Catherine said of the Miraculous Medal, "I believe that the good God will be glorified and the Blessed Virgin honored; it will give new fervor to all hearts." The medal depicted Mary as she appeared to Catherine, surrounded by the invocation that has become known throughout the world, "O Mary conceived without sin, pray for us who have recourse to thee."

Virgin Mother of God, Mary Immaculate, we unite ourselves to you under your title of Our Lady of the Miraculous Medal. May this medal be for each one of us a sure sign of your motherly affection for us and a constant reminder of our filial duties towards you. While wearing it, may we be blessed by your loving protection and preserved in the grace of your Son. Most powerful Virgin, Mother of our Savior, keep us close to you every moment of our

lives so that like you we may live and act according to the teaching and example of your Son. Obtain for us, your children, the grace of a happy death so that in union with you we may enjoy the happiness of heaven forever. Amen.

DAY FORTY-TWO
Frances Crane Lillie's Mary Garden

During the Middle Ages, countless flowers were associated with Our Lady. Honeysuckle was Our Lady's Fingers; harebell was Our Lady's Thimble; forget-me-nots were Mary's Eyes; morning glories were Our Lady's Mantle; spiderwort was Our Lady's Tears.

In 1932 Frances Crane Lillie, a summer resident of Cape Cod and a convert to Catholicism, planted a garden of flowers associated with Mary (as well as other saints), and then donated the garden to St. Joseph's Church in Woods Hole. For the better appreciation of visitors to the garden, Frances published a pamphlet that listed the common names for the flowers and plants beside the old religious names. She entitled her pamphlet, *Our Lady in Her Garden*, and included an especially appropriate invocation from the Litany of the Blessed Virgin, "*Rosa Mystica, ora pro nobis,* Mystical Rose, pray for us."

Frances's work on the garden took four years, despite the help of professional landscape architect Dorothea K. Harrison, and was completed in 1937. "We found some five hundred [plants and flowers] named after Her," Frances wrote in her pamphlet, "three hundred and fifty after the Saints, and about one hundred [other plants with religious significance]."

Frances Crane Lillie died in 1958, but St. Joseph's parish has kept up her garden. Today, Mary's Gardens organization helps amateurs and professionals plant their own Mary Garden. Visit them at http://www.mgardens.org.

> They shall return and
> dwell beneath my shadow,
> they shall flourish as a garden;
> they shall blossom as the vine,
> their fragrance shall be like
> the wine of Lebanon.
> —*Hosea 14:7*

DAY FORTY-THREE
Pius XII and the feast of the Immaculate Heart of Mary

Reverence for the pure heart of Mary goes back to the birth of Christ, when Mary, marveling over everything that had happened to her, "kept all these things, pondering them in her heart" (Lk. 2:19). St. Bernardine of Siena compared Mary's heart to "a furnace of Divine Love." St. John Eudes said, "Next to the Heart of God, there never was and never shall be a heart so good, liberal, benevolent, magnificent, and so replete with kindness as the most admirable Heart of Mary." In fact, it was John Eudes who in 1643 first celebrated a feast day in honor of the Heart of Mary.

The appearances of Our Lady to the children at Fatima in 1917 renewed interest in devotion to the Immaculate Heart of Mary, the heart that loved God completely, never gave into a sinful impulse, and is filled with love and compassion for all of us. In 1942, to mark the twenty-fifth anniversary of the visions at Fatima, Pope Pius XII consecrated the world to Mary's Immaculate Heart, and assigned August 22 as her feast day.

At that time, the feast was still an optional observance.

Then, on May 4, 1944, Pope Pius made the feast of the Immaculate Heart of Mary an obligatory liturgical celebration for the church throughout the world, meaning that he believed the spiritual benefits of contemplating the pure and holy Heart of Mary should be encouraged among all the faithful.

Holy Immaculate Mary, help all who are in trouble. Give courage to the faint-hearted, console the sad, heal the infirm, pray for the people, intercede for the clergy, have a special care for nuns; may all feel, all enjoy your kind and powerful assistance, all who now and always render and will render, you honor, and will offer you their petitions. Hear all our prayers, O Mother, and grant them all. We are all your children: Grant the prayers of your children. Amen.
—*Blessed Pope John XXIII*

The expedition of Sebastian Vizcaino

In the sixteenth century Spanish merchants traveled back and forth across the Pacific Ocean between Spain's colonies in the Philippines and Mexico. It was a long voyage that was often hard on the ships and their crew. Members of the colonial government in Mexico became interested in establishing a Spanish settlement in a safe harbor along the California coast, where ships from the Philippines could put in for repairs and the sailors could rest and restock their supplies of food and fresh water.

In 1602 the Viceroy of New Spain chose Sebastian Vizcaino, an experienced commander and merchant who had made the voyage across the Pacific many times, to lead an expedition of discovery up the California coast in search of a suitable harbor. On May 5, 1602, Vizcaino placed himself, his men, and their mission under the protection of Our Lady of Mount Carmel. Then they sailed out of the harbor of Acapulco to explore California. By turning to Mary for help, Vizcaino joined a long line of explorers who placed themselves under her protection, beginning with Christopher Columbus, who sailed to the New World aboard a ship christened *Santa Maria*, or *St. Mary*. When Spanish settlers moved into California they named every town they founded after Our Lady or a saint. It's not going too far to say that devotion to Mary and to the saints was literally the bedrock of early California.

Upon his return to Mexico in 1603, Vizcaino encouraged the Spanish to settle in two especially favorable locations—the harbor of what is now San Diego and the harbor at Monterrey.

O most beautiful flower of Mt. Carmel, fruitful vine, splendor of Heaven. Blessed Mother of the Son of God, Immaculate Virgin, assist me in my necessity, O Star of the Sea, help me and show me here you are my Mother. O Holy Mary, Mother of God, queen of Heaven and Earth, I humbly beseech you from the bottom of my heart to succor me in my necessity [make request]. There are none who can withstand your power.

DAY FORTY-FIVE
The devotion of St. John Damascene to Our Lady

S he has captivated my spirit," St. John Damascene said of Mary. "Day and night I see her in my imagination."

As his name suggests, John was born in Damascus, where his father and his grandfather, in spite of their Christian faith, had been high-ranking administrators in the caliph's government. When a new caliph came to power and instituted a series of anti-Christian measures, John left his home for Jerusalem, where he first became a monk, then a priest. In the Holy City he gained a reputation as a brilliant preacher, as well as an inspired composer of hymns. He tends to be celebrated for his defense of the veneration of sacred images during the Iconoclast period, when extremist elements in the East rampaged through churches, destroying all representations of Our Lord, Our Lady, and the saints. But, out of his deep love for Mary, he also wrote eloquently about her. "If nothing glorifies God more than mercy," St. John wrote, "who will deny that His mother is blessed with that virtue.... She is the furnisher of all good things."

John helped develop the theology of Our Lady's Assumption—that after her time on earth had ended, God raised Mary, body and soul, to heaven—and he was an early promoter of the doctrine of Mary's Immaculate Conception— that Mary was conceived in the womb of her mother, St. Anne, without original sin. St. John was also a staunch defender of the doctrine that Mary can truly be called the Theotokos, or the Mother of God.

O daughter of Joachim and Anna, and Lady, receive the prayer of a sinful servant, but one who, nonetheless, loves and cherishes you ardently, holds you as his only hope of joy, the guardian of his life, his intercessor with your Son, and sure pledge of salvation.
—*Prayer of St. John Damascene*

Pope John XXII and the evening bells of Rome

Three times a day, when the Angelus bell rings out from Catholic church steeples, we are urged to pause and recall the great miracle when "the Word was made flesh and dwelt among us" (Jn. 1:14). The custom is an old one, dating back at least eight hundred years when in various parts of Europe, as the evening bell rang, Catholics would say three Hail Marys in honor of the annunciation to Mary and the incarnation of Jesus Christ.

Pope John XXII gave the custom new impetus when he encouraged Catholics in Rome to adopt the practice of reciting three Hail Marys at the end of the workday. The tradition of reciting the Hail Marys at the beginning of the day and again at noon evolved over time. And the Angelus as we know it today, with its verses from the Gospels of St. Luke and St. John and its concluding prayer, achieved its final form in Italy in 1612.

In 1851, when the custom of praying the Angelus was well-established, Blessed Pope Pius IX urged the faithful to turn to Mary every day. "She is the best of Mothers," he wrote, "our safest confidant and in fact the very motive of our hope: she obtains all she asks for and her prayer is always heard."

The angel of the Lord declared unto Mary.
And she conceived of the Holy Spirit.
Hail Mary.
Behold the handmaid of the Lord.
Be it done unto me according thy word.
Hail Mary.
The Word was made flesh.
And dwelt among us.
Hail Mary.
Pray for us, O Holy Mother of God.
That we may be made worthy of the promises of Christ.

Let us pray.
Pour forth, we beseech Thee, O Lord, Thy grace into our hearts. That we to whom the Incarnation of Thy Son was made known by the message of an angel, may, by His Passion and Cross, be brought the glory of His Resurrection. Through the same Christ our Lord. Amen.

DAY FORTY-SEVEN
Our Lady of Lujan

In 1630 a Brazilian sculptor was commissioned to make an image of the Blessed Virgin in terra-cotta for a church in Argentina. When the sculpture was finished, the statue was packed carefully in a wooden crate and loaded into the back of an ox cart for the long journey to its new home. According to the legend, at the Lujan River the oxen stopped and refused to move. The teamsters assumed that it was a sign, that Mary wanted her image venerated at Lujan.

A wealthy gentleman named Don Rosendo took charge of the statue and built a shrine for it on his land. It remained in the Rosendo family's private chapel for forty years and in 1685 was transferred to a large shrine church where more pilgrims would have access to the sacred image. Today the statue, dressed in elaborate robes of white and sky blue (the colors of the Argentine flag) is enshrined a grand nineteenth-century basilica.

In 1998 Pope John Paul II came to the Argentinean community's national church in Rome to enthrone a copy of the statue of Our Lady of

Lujan. The Holy Father composed this prayer for the occasion:

Our Lady of Lujan, help the people of Argentina, support them in their defense of life, console them in their suffering, accompany them in their joys and always help them to raise their eyes to heaven, where the colors of their flag blend with the colors of your immaculate mantle. To you, the Church's honor and praise forever, Mother of Jesus and our Mother!

Mother Maria Theresa of Jesus, founder of the School Sisters of Notre Dame

"All the works of God proceed slowly and in pain," Mother Maria Theresa of Jesus wrote, "but then their roots are the sturdier and their flowering the lovelier."

Many religious orders begin out of a desire to serve a need or solve a problem; Mother Maria Theresa (born Caroline Gerhardinger) began her community, the School Sister of Notre Dame, to revive Catholic education in Bavaria, where it had been banned by the government for twenty years. As the order's name implies, dedication to schoolchildren and devotion to Our Lady were the cornerstones of Mother Maria Theresa's order; she designed a curriculum that taught secular subjects and Catholic principles.

About the same time that the School Sisters were founded, waves of German, Austrian, and Bohemian Catholics were emigrating to the United States. Now Mother Maria Theresa saw a fresh challenge—to give German-speaking children an education, to help them assimilate into American society, and to keep them firmly rooted in their Catholic faith. In 1847 she sent the first five School Sisters to the United States, led by Sister Caroline Friess. The order thrived in the United States. Mother Maria Theresa could not keep up with requests from American bishops for more sisters, but the order was beginning to win recruits from the daughters of Catholic immigrants in America, which could fulfill the need.

At the time of Mother Maria Theresa's death there were 2,500 School Sisters of Notre Dame in Europe and the Americas. But as Monsignor Adalbert Kuhn said at Mother's funeral Mass, "It was not the greatness of the number of her sisters that delighted her, but their inward transformation to the image and likeness of the crucified Son of God."

I lift up my eyes to the hills.
From whence does my help come?
My help comes from the LORD,
who made heaven and earth.
—*Psalm 121:1–2*

Murals of St. Joan of Arc are discovered in
her favorite shrine to Our Lady, 1997

Ashort walk from St. Joan of Arc's house in the village of Domremy, France, stands a small chapel dedicated to Our Lady of Bermont. Although the shrine dates back to the eleventh century, it never became a famous destination for pilgrims; it is now what it always has been— a favorite place of prayer for the people of the neighboring farms and villages.

One of the most faithful visitors to the chapel was St. Joan of Arc. As a girl, she came almost every Saturday to pray before the lovely wooden sculpture of the Virgin and Child. Incredibly, the little chapel where St. Joan prayed and the image of Our Lady that she loved have both survived. The original statue is enshrined today in the Basilica of St. Joan in Domremy; a replica stands in the chapel of Our Lady of Bermont.

In 1997, during some routine repair and restoration work inside the chapel, workmen discovered under an old coat of whitewash two wall paintings of a young girl. In one painting the girl is shown wearing the traditional dress of a woman from the Domremy region as she kneels in prayer. In the second painting the girl is shown wearing men's clothes. One of the things we know about St. Joan is after she began her mission to liberate France from the English, she put aside the dresses and aprons she would have worn at home and wore a man's tunic and hose. Some historians believe these two paintings inside St. Joan's favorite shrine are portraits of her made shortly after her death.

During her trial, one of St. Joan's interrogators accused her of calling upon evil spirits to help her, but Joan rejected this charge and maintained her orthodoxy. "I beg Our Lord and Our Lady to send me their counsel and comfort," she said, "and then they send it to me."

While I was still young, before I went on my travels, I sought wisdom openly in my prayer. Before the temple I asked for her, and I will search for her to the last.
My heart was stirred to seek her, therefore I have gained a good possession. The Lord gave me a tongue as my reward, and I will praise him with it.
—*Sirach 51:13–14, 21–22*

DAY OF PENTECOST
Mary, Mother of the Church

After Christ's ascension into heaven, the Blessed Virgin Mary, St. Mary Magdalen, and the apostles retired to the room that had been the scene of the Last Supper to await the coming of the Holy Spirit with nine days of prayer—this was the church's first novena. In the morning, to the sound of a mighty rushing wind, the Holy Spirit descended on them all in the form of small flames of fire that appeared over the heads of everyone in the room. As a large crowd gathered outside the house, St. Peter went to speak to them and proclaim that Jesus Christ was the Savior foretold by the prophets of ancient Israel. When he had finished speaking, three thousand people asked to be baptized.

Pentecost is the day the grace of the Holy Spirit came down upon Mary and the disciples; it is the occasion of the first Christian sermon, it is the anniversary of the first great conversion— it is the birthday of the church. And at the center of this day is Mary. She became Mother of God in the stable in Bethlehem, the Mother of Sorrows at the foot of the cross, now with all the apostles and disciples gathered around her, she becomes Mother of the Church. And she is one thing more: Mary is the ideal of what all Christians are called to be. While all members of the church strive to become perfect as our Father in heaven is perfect, she is the model of perfect holiness. The angel Gabriel himself declared this when at the Annunciation he greeted Mary as "full of grace."

Blessed and venerable are you, O Virgin Mary, who without spot to your maiden-hood, were made Mother of the Savior. O Virgin Mother of God, He Whom the whole world cannot contain, enclosed Himself in your womb, becoming Man. Alleluia, alleluia. After childbirth you remained a pure virgin. O Mother of God, intercede for us. Alleluia.

ABOUT PARACLETE PRESS

Who We Are

Paraclete Press is an ecumenical publisher of books and recordings on Christian spirituality. Our publishing represents a full expression of Christian belief and practice—from Catholic to Evangelical, from Protestant to Orthodox.

Paraclete Press is the publishing arm of the Community of Jesus, an ecumenical monastic community in the Benedictine tradition. As such, we are uniquely positioned in the marketplace without connection to a large corporation and with informal relationships to many branches and denominations of faith.

We like it best when people buy our books from booksellers, our partners in successfully reaching as wide an audience as possible.

What We Are Doing

Books

Paraclete Press publishes books that show the richness and depth of what it means to be Christian. Although Benedictine spirituality is at the heart of all that we do, we publish books that reflect the Christian experience across many cultures, time periods, and houses of worship.

We publish books that nourish the vibrant life of the church and its people—books about spiritual practice, formation, history, ideas, and customs.

We have several different series of books within Paraclete Press, including the best-selling Living Library series of modernized classic texts; A Voice from the Monastery—giving voice to men and women monastics about what it means to live a spiritual life today; award-winning literary faith fiction; and books that explore Judaism and Islam and discover how these faiths inform Christian thought and practice.

Recordings

From Gregorian chant to contemporary American choral works, our music recordings celebrate the richness of sacred choral music through the centuries. Paraclete is proud to distribute the recordings of the internationally acclaimed choir Gloriæ Dei Cantores, who have been praised for their "rapt and fathomless spiritual intensity" by *American Record Guide*, and the Gloriæ Dei Cantores Schola, which specializes in the study and performance of Gregorian chant. Paraclete is also the exclusive North American distributor of the recordings of the Monastic Choir of St. Peter's Abbey in Solesmes, France, long considered to be a leading authority on Gregorian chant performance.

Learn more about us at our Web site:
www.paracletepress.com,
or call us toll-free at 1-800-451-5006.